Annual Survey

US Government & Politics

Anthony J. Bennett

Philip Allan Updates, an imprint of Hodder Education, an Hachette UK company, Market Place, Deddington, Oxfordshire OX15 0SE

Orders
Bookpoint Ltd, 130 Milton Park, Abingdon, Oxfordshire OX14 4SB
tel: 01235 827827
fax: 01235 400401
e-mail: education@bookpoint.co.uk

Lines are open 9.00 a.m.–5.00 p.m., Monday to Saturday, with a 24-hour message answering service. You can also order through the Philip Allan Updates website: www.philipallan.co.uk

ISBN 978-1-4441-3772-9

First published 2011
Impression number   5   4   3   2   1
Year   2015   2014   2013   2012   2011

Printed by MPG Books, Bodmin

Hachette UK's policy is to use papers that are natural, renewable and recyclable products and made from wood grown in sustainable forests. The logging and manufacturing processes are expected to conform to the environmental regulations of the country of origin.

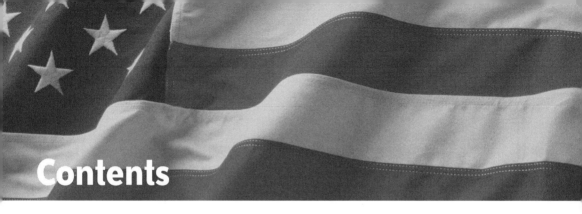

Contents

Chapter 1

The 2010 mid-term congressional elections

What you need to know

- Mid-term congressional elections come halfway through a president's 4-year term of office.
- Therefore, they fall in years 2002, 2006, 2010 and so on.
- In these years, there are elections for all 435 members of the House of Representatives and one-third of the Senate.
- The president's party usually loses seats in both houses in mid-term elections.

Before the 2010 mid-term elections, the Democrats controlled both the House and the Senate. They had a 77-seat majority in the House (with 256 Democrats to 179 Republicans) and an 18-seat majority in the Senate (with 59 Democrats to 41 Republicans). The Republicans therefore needed to make an overall gain of 39 seats in the House and 10 seats in the Senate to become the majority party in either chamber. Writing in last year's *Annual Survey*, we concluded that 'the Democrats will remain in control of both houses of Congress following the 2010 mid-term elections'. By the time Election Day came round on 2 November 2010, it was all but certain that the Democrats would lose control of the House and might even struggle to keep control of the Senate. So what happened and why?

The primaries

It is usually exceedingly difficult to defeat incumbent members of Congress during the primaries. In the five election cycles between 2000 and 2008, an average of fewer than four House members and one senator were defeated in the primaries. The 2010 cycle was above average in both chambers and significantly so in the Senate, where three incumbents lost at the nomination stage — the highest figure since four were defeated in the primaries in 1980.

In the House, two Democrats and two Republicans lost in the primaries: Democrats Alan Mollohan in West Virginia and Carolyn Cheeks Kilpatrick in Michigan; Republicans Bob Inglis in South Carolina and Parker Griffith in Alabama. Mollohan, a 14-term House veteran, had been mired in ethical problems for the past 3 years. The Democrats narrowly lost the seat in November. Kilpatrick, first elected in 1996 from a black-majority district, and a prominent member of the congressional black caucus, had been dogged by a scandal concerning her son's involvement in a text messaging sex scandal. Inglis was defeated by Trey Gowdy, who criticised Inglis for what he claimed was an overly-moderate voting record. Inglis had opposed the Iraq war troop surge in 2007 and supported the bank bailout package in 2008. Gowdy went on to win 64% of the vote in the general election to hold the seat for the Republicans. Parker Griffith had switched parties to become a Republican in late 2009, but Republicans in his Alabama district wanted a life-long Republican on the ballot in November, not some newcomer.

One of the three senators to lose at the nomination stage was also a party switcher — Arlen Specter of Pennsylvania — who had switched from the Republicans to the Democrats in mid-2009. Specter had fallen out with Pennsylvania Republicans for what many of them regarded as his liberal voting record over many years. Specter lost the Democratic primary to Congressman Joe Sestak, who went on to lose in the general election to Republican Patrick Toomey. Senator Bob Bennett of Utah also found himself ousted for being insufficiently conservative. Bennett didn't even make it to the primary, being denied a place in the Utah Republican Senate primary at the Republican state convention. This was one of a number of elections influenced by Tea Party activists (see Chapter 8). Another was the senate race in Alaska, where incumbent Lisa Murkowski lost in the Republican Primary to Joe Miller, who was backed by the Tea Party movement and Sarah Palin. But Murkowski refused to bow out, fought the general election as a write-in candidate — and won. More of that anon.

The Senate results

An unusually high number of Senate seats were contested in 2010 — 37 in all — the most since 1962 (see Table 1.1 on p. 7) There were the 34 seats last contested in 2004, plus three special elections to fill up the remaining years of senators who had either retired or died. The Democrats were defending 19 of these 37 seats. It was, therefore, from just those 19 seats that the Republicans had to make their overall gain of 10 seats if they were to win back the Senate majority that they had lost in 2006. It was a tall order, and in the end they made an overall gain of just six seats, defeating two Democrat incumbents and winning four of the Democrat's seven open seats. They held all their 18 seats, including all six open seats in Florida, Kansas, Kentucky, Missouri, New Hampshire and Ohio.

The two Democrat incumbents to go down on Election Day were one-term Blanche Lincoln in Arkansas and four-term Russell Feingold in Wisconsin. Lincoln's defeat was expected. She struggled even to win the Democratic Senate primary, winning only 44% of the vote in a three-way race. Having failed to get over 50%, she had to then face a run-off against her nearest challenger, Bill Halter. Even in the run-off, she managed only 52% of the vote to Halter's 48%. So by the time she faced Republican Congressman John Boozman in November, Lincoln was both damaged goods and low on resources. She lost by 21 percentage points to Boozman, gaining a mere 37% of the vote — the worst ever result for an incumbent senator.

Feingold's defeat was not expected early on in the election cycle. He had won re-election to his fourth term in 2004 by a comfortable 12 percentage-point margin in a year that was not particularly kind to Democrats. Feingold will be best remembered for his co-authorship — with Republican Senator John McCain of Arizona — of the 2002 Bipartisan Campaign Reform Act, often referred to as the McCain–Feingold Act. In 2008, Senator Feingold had even toyed with a bid for the Democratic presidential nomination. But now in 2010, he went down to businessman Ron Johnson 52–47.

The Republicans won four open seats from the Democrats — Illinois, Indiana, North Dakota and Pennsylvania. All but North Dakota were states that Obama had won in 2008; indeed, in Illinois the Republicans won Obama's former Senate seat. Although an overall gain of six seats was impressive, it might have been better but for the influence of Tea Party activists at the nomination stage in Delaware, Colorado and Nevada.

In Delaware, the Republicans had been pretty certain to win the seat vacated in 2008 by Joe Biden when he was elected vice-president. The temporary appointee Ted Kaufman announced that he would not run for election in 2010. With the Republicans almost certain to nominate Congressman — and former state governor — Mike Castle, even Biden's son, Beau, decided to give the race a pass. But then Castle lost in the Republican primary to Tea Party-backed Christine O'Donnell, who went on to lose the November race 56–40.

In Colorado, Democrat Michael Bennet was running for his first full term, having been appointed to the seat in 2009 following Senator Ken Salazar's appointment as President Obama's secretary of the interior. Bennet, who had never run an election campaign in his life, was seen as vulnerable to the expected Republican candidate, former Lieutenant Governor Jane Norton. But Norton lost in the Republican primary to another Tea Party favourite Ken Buck. Buck went on to lose in a tight race in November.

In Nevada, Senate Majority Leader Harry Reid was regarded as highly vulnerable for re-election and was expecting a tough fight against expected Republican candidate Sue Lowden, the chair of the Nevada state Republican Party. But Lowden lost in the Republican primary to Tea Party-backed Sharron Angle. Angle ran a controversial and chaotic campaign in the general election which resulted in Reid holding his seat by a comfortable five percentage points.

And then there was the Senate race in Alaska, where Lisa Murkowski was running for her second full term. She lost in the Republican primary to Joe Miller, who had received endorsements both from former state governor and

Table 1.1 Results of Senate elections, 2010

State	Winner	Party	%	Opponent	Party	%
Alabama	**Richard Shelby**	R	65	William Barnes	Dem	35
Alaska	**Lisa Murkowski**	Write-in	39	Joe Miller	R	35
				Scott McAdams	Dem	23
Arizona	**John McCain**	R	59	Rodney Glassman	Dem	35
Arkansas	John Boozman	R	58	**Blanche Lincoln**	Dem	37
California	**Barbara Boxer**	Dem	52	Carly Fiorina	R	43
Colorado	**Michael Bennet**	Dem	48	Ken Buck	R	47
Connecticut	*Richard Blumenthal	Dem	54	Linda McMahon	R	44
†Delaware	*Christopher Coons	Dem	57	Christine O'Donnell	R	40
Florida	*Marco Rubio	R	49	Charlie Crist	Ind	30
Georgia	**Johnny Isakson**	R	58	Michael Thurmond	Dem	39
Hawaii	**Daniel Inouye**	Dem	75	Cam Cavasso	R	22
Idaho	**Michael Crapo**	R	71	Tom Sullivan	Dem	25
Illinois	Mark Kirk	R	48	*Alexi Giannoulias	Dem	46
Indiana	Daniel Coats	R	55	*Brad Ellsworth	Dem	40
Iowa	**Charles Grassley**	R	65	Roxanne Conlin	Dem	33
Kansas	*Jerry Moran	R	70	Lisa Johnston	Dem	26
Kentucky	*Rand Paul	R	56	Jack Conway	Dem	44
Louisiana	**David Vitter**	R	57	Charlie Melancon	Dem	38
Maryland	**Barbara Mikulski**	Dem	62	Eric Wargotz	R	36
Missouri	*Roy Blunt	R	54	Robin Carnahan	Dem	41
Nevada	**Harry Reid**	Dem	50	Sharron Angle	R	45
New Hampshire	*Kelly Ayotte	R	60	Paul Hodes	Dem	37
New York	**Charles Schumer**	Dem	65	Jay Townsend	R	33
‡New York	**Kirsten Gillibrand**	Dem	61	Joseph DioGuardi	R	37
North Carolina	**Richard Burr**	R	55	Elaine Marshall	Dem	43
North Dakota	John Hoeven	R	76	*Tracy Potter	Dem	22
Ohio	*Rob Portman	R	57	Lee Fisher	Dem	39
Oklahoma	**Tom Coburn**	R	70	Jim Rogers	Dem	26
Oregon	**Ron Wyden**	Dem	56	Jim Huffman	R	40
Pennsylvania	Pat Toomey	R	51	*Joe Sestak	Dem	49
South Carolina	**Jim DeMint**	R	62	Alvin Greene	Dem	28
South Dakota	**John Thune**	R	100	[Unopposed]	—	—
Utah	*Mike Lee	R	62	Sam Granato	Dem	33
Vermont	**Patrick Leahy**	Dem	65	Len Britton	R	31
Washington	**Patty Murray**	Dem	52	Dino Rossi	R	48
•West Virginia	*Joe Manchin	Dem	54	John Raese	R	43
Wisconsin	Ron Johnson	R	52	**Russell Feingold**	Dem	47

Incumbents in bold

* Incumbent party candidate in open seat

† Special election to fill the remaining 4 years of the term to which Joe Biden was elected in 2008

‡ Special election to fill the remaining 2 years of the term to which Hillary Clinton was elected in 2006

• Special election to fill the remaining 2 years of the term to which Robert Byrd was elected in 2006

2008 Republican vice-presidential candidate Sarah Palin and from the Tea Party movement. Murkowski then ran against Miller and his Democrat opponent

Scott McAdams as a write-in candidate. This meant that Murkowski's name did not appear on the ballot paper; her supporters had to write it in and then vote for her. Murkowski held the seat, winning 39% of the vote to Miller's 35% and McAdams' 23%. This was the first time that a senator had been elected as a write-in candidate since Strom Thurmond of South Carolina in 1954. Murkowski will sit in the new Congress as a Republican.

The party balance in the new Senate will therefore be 53 Democrats and 47 Republicans. Of the 25 senators who sought re-election, 21 (84%) were re-elected (see Table 1.2). The average re-election rate in the Senate between 1990 and 2008 was 87%, so 2010 was pretty much in line with recent election cycles. That could certainly not be said of what occurred in the House of Representatives.

Table 1.2 Senators: retired, defeated, re-elected, 1990–2010

Year	Retired	Sought re-election	Defeated in primary	Defeated in general election	Total re-elected	% re-elected who sought re-election
1990	3	32	0	1	31	96.9
1992	7	28	1	4	23	82.1
1994	9	26	0	2	24	92.3
1996	13	21	1	1	19	90.5
1998	5	29	0	3	26	89.6
2000	5	29	0	5	24	82.8
2002	5	28	1	3	24	85.7
2004	8	26	0	1	25	96.1
2006	4	29	1	6	23	79.3
2008	5	30	0	5	25	83.3
2010	12	25	3†	2	21	84.0

† Senator Lisa Murkowski lost in the Republican primary in Alaska but won in the general election as a write-in candidate

The House results

Of the 396 House members who sought re-election, 338 (85%) were re-elected, the lowest re-election rate since 1946 (see Table 1.3). The overall loss of 63 seats by the president's party — including 52 incumbents on Election Day — makes this the worst mid-term performance by the president's party 2 years into a presidential term since the Republicans lost 75 seats in 1922 (see Table 1.4). The average re-election rate in the House between 1990 and 2008 was 95%, so 2010 saw a significantly lower rate of re-election than in previous cycles. Indeed, almost as many House members (54) were defeated in the 2010 general election as were defeated in all the four general elections between 2002 and 2008 put together (55).

Among the Democrat casualties were some very senior congressmen, including three standing committee chairmen with 98 years of congressional service between them: James Oberstar of Minnesota (chairman of the Transportation and Infrastructure Committee); Ike Skelton of Missouri (chairman of the Armed Services Committee); and John Spratt of North Carolina (chairman of the Budget Committee).

Table 1.3 House members: retired, defeated, re-elected, 1990–2010

Year	Retired	Sought re-election	Defeated in primary	Defeated in general election	Total re-elected	% re-elected who sought re-election
1990	27	407	1	15	391	96.1
1992	67	368	19	24	325	88.3
1994	48	387	4	34	349	90.2
1996	50	383	2	21	360	94.0
1998	33	401	1	6	394	98.3
2000	32	403	3	6	394	97.8
2002	38	397	8	8	381	96.0
2004	29	404	2	7	395	97.8
2006	28	405	2	21	382	94.3
2008	32	402	4	19	379	94.3
2010	37	396	4	54	338	85.4

Table 1.4 Losses by president's party in mid-term elections 2 years into a presidential term, 1914–2010

Year	President	Party	Gains/losses by president's party in	
			Senate	House
1914	Woodrow Wilson	Dem	+5	−59
1922	Warren Harding	R	−8	−75
1930	Herbert Hoover	R	−8	−49
1934	Franklin Roosevelt	Dem	+10	+9
1946	Harry Truman	Dem	−12	−45
1954	Dwight Eisenhower	R	−1	−18
1962	John Kennedy	Dem	+3	−4
1970	Richard Nixon	R	+2	−12
1978	Jimmy Carter	Dem	−5	−15
1982	Ronald Reagan	R	+1	−26
1990	George H. W. Bush	R	−1	−8
1994	Bill Clinton	Dem	−8	−52
2002	George W. Bush	R	+2	+5
2010	Barack Obama	Dem	−6	−63

But these were the exception. Of the 52 House Democrats who lost on Election Day, 36 (69%) had been elected in or since 2006, and a further 4 (8%) had been elected in either 2002 or 2004. Twenty-three (44%) of the 52 defeated had served only one term. So what the Republicans were largely doing in 2010 was regaining many of the seats that they had lost in 2006 and 2008 — the years when President George W. Bush, a declining economy and an unpopular war had damaged the Republican brand.

This reclaiming of old territory by the Republicans can also be seen by studying the fate of the so-called McCain-Democrats in the House. By McCain-Democrats we mean Democrat House members whose district voted for Republican presidential candidate John McCain in 2008. Of the 46 McCain Democrats in the House in November 2010, six retired — and all six open seats were won by the Republicans. Alan Mollohan was defeated in his primary — and the Republicans won the open seat in November. That left 39 McCain-Democrats on Election Day, of whom 28 (72%) lost and only 11 won.

Of those 11 McCain-Democrats who won, 9 had voted 'no' on the final passage of Obama's healthcare reform bill earlier in the year. The two who had voted 'yes' on healthcare reform but who still won both saw their share of the vote drop dramatically: Nick Rahall in West Virginia down from 67% in 2008 to 55%; Gabrielle Giffords in Arizona down from 55% to 48%. Of the 30 of the 34 House Democrats who voted 'no' on healthcare reform and sought re-election, 4 retired and 17 (57%) lost. Omitting Steve Lynch of Massachusetts, who voted 'no' on healthcare because he didn't think the reforms went far enough, the remaining 12 saw their share of the vote fall by an average of just under 12 percentage points. Mike Ross of Arkansas had his vote cut from 86% in 2008 to just 57% in 2010.

The party balance in the new House of Representatives is 242 Republicans and 193 Democrats. That is the most House members that the Republicans have had since the 245 they had following the mid-term elections in 1946.

Who voted for whom and why?

By comparing the exit polls from 2008 with 2010 we can see how voting patterns for the Democrats among key groups have shifted in those 2 years. The right-hand column of Table 1.5 shows that the Democrats lost support among almost every voting group. Only Democrats and liberals gave them a higher share of the vote this time. But where had the Democrats particularly and critically lost support? We can identify three key groups: independents; those living in the Midwest; and young voters.

In both the 2006 and 2008 House elections, independent voters had given the majority of their votes to Democratic candidates, splitting 57–39 in 2006 and 52–43 in 2008. But in 2010, independents split 38–56 in favour of Republican House candidates, a fall of 14 percentage points for the Democrats. Independent voters had deserted Obama because they perceived that he had campaigned as the candidate of 'change' but governed as a president of 'more of the same' — more big government spending, more

Table 1.5 Who voted for whom: comparison of 2008 and 2010

Category (percentage of voters)	Democrat vote 2008 (%)	Democrat vote 2010 (%)	Change in Democrat vote (% points)
Male (47)	49	42	–7
Women (53)	56	48	–8
White (78)	43	37	–6
African-American (10)	95	90	–5
Latino (8)	67	64	–3
White men (37)	41	35	–6
White women (41)	46	40	–6
Black men (4)	95	85	–10
Black women (6)	96	93	–3
Aged 18–29 (11)	**66**	**57**	**–9**
Aged 30–44 (23)	52	47	–5
Aged 45–59 (44)	50	†	†
Aged 60+ (23)	45	†	†
All Protestant (54)	45	39	–6
White Protestant (44)	34	29	–5
Catholic (25)	54	44	–10
Democrats (36)	89	92	+3
Republicans (36)	9	4	–5
Independents (28)	**52**	**38**	**–14**
Liberal (20)	89	90	+1
Moderate (39)	60	55	–5
Conservative (41)	20	14	–6
Northeast (21)	59	54	–5
Midwest (26)	**54**	**44**	**–10**
South (20)	45	39	–6
West (23)	57	49	–8
Urban (30)	63	56	–7
Suburbs (50)	50	43	–7
Rural (20)	45	38	–7
Family income			
$30–50,000 (19)	55	51	–4
$50–75,000 (21)	48	46	–2
$75–100,000 (16)	51	42	–9
$100–200,000 (19)	48	42	–6
Over $200,000 (7)	52	35	–17
2008 voters			
Obama	—	84	—
McCain	—	7	—
Others	—	33	—
Didn't vote	—	38	—

Source: www.cnn.com/ELECTION/2010/results/polls

† Exit polls in 2010 used different age groupings from those used in 2008

congressional earmarks on legislation, more liberal policies, too much time spent on healthcare reform and far too little on boosting a stagnant economy and creating jobs. It almost now seems to be true that winning the vote of independents is the key to winning national elections. As Bob Benenson perceptively wrote in *CQ Weekly* ('Pendulum pushed well to the right', 8 November 2010):

> The prominence of this frustrated and relatively non-ideological amalgamation of voters in tipping national elections will require both parties to navigate a minefield of difficult strategic and tactical decisions over the next couple of years.

Just as key to winning elections is the Midwest — the bellwether region of US politics. The Democrats' share of the vote in the Midwest rose from 48% in 2004 to 52% in 2006, and to 54% in 2008. In 2010, their share here dropped 10 percentage points to just 44%. They lost four Midwestern Senate seats — Illinois, Indiana, North Dakota and Wisconsin — which meant that the Republicans won all eight Senate seats that were up for election in the region. In the seven races which the Democrats contested — they didn't even bother putting up a candidate in South Dakota — their candidates received an average vote of just 37%. It was just as disastrous in the House races where they lost a total of 19 seats, including five in Ohio and four in Illinois. For Ronald Brownstein writing his post-election column in the *National Journal*, this constitutes a 'heartland headache' for the Democrats and Obama for 2012. 'Democrats have to be more competitive in states that don't touch an ocean if they want to bounce back', wrote Brownstein.

The collapse of the Democrat vote among younger voters must be another major concern for the party and the president. Not only did the Democrats' share of the 18–29-year-old vote drop by nine percentage points, but whereas in 2008 this age group made up 18% of voters, in 2010 they were only 11%. It was a double whammy: fewer votes from fewer voters.

When analysing why people voted as they did, the key factors appear to be threefold: President Obama, the economy, and perceptions about the role of the federal government. The 44% of voters who approved of how Obama is handling his job as president (see Figure 1.1) split 85–13 for the Democrats. But the 52% of those who disapproved split 11–86 for the Republicans. Indeed, of the 40% who strongly disapproved of Obama's job as president, a whopping 92% voted Republican. Furthermore, 61% of voters said that Obama was a factor in their voting. It was much the same when asked about the president's policies. Of the 43% who thought they would help the country, 87% voted Democrat; of the 52% who thought they would hurt the country, 89% voted Republican.

Figure 1.1 Do you approve or disapprove of the way Barack Obama is handling his job as president?

■ Approve
■ Disapprove

All voters: 44% / 52%
Republicans: 6% / 91%
Independents: 35% / 60%
Democrats: 84% / 12%

Source: Resurgent Republic–Democracy Corps Post-election Survey, 2–3 November 2010

When asked 'What is the most important issue facing the country today?', 62% of voters said it was the economy — almost identical to the 63% who answered the same question the same way in 2008. But whereas those 2008 voters split 53–44 for the Democrats, in 2010 they split 54–44 for the Republicans. Asked 'Do you think the condition of the nation's economy is excellent, good, not good or poor?', only 10% chose 'excellent' or 'good', with 89% choosing 'not good' or 'poor'. Again, the figures had hardly moved from 2008. But whereas in 2008 those saying the nation's economy was 'not good' or 'poor' split 54–44 for the Democrats, in 2010 they split 56–41 for the Republicans.

Broaden this out to the question 'Do you think things in this country today are on the right track or on the wrong track?' and 26% said 'right track' while 66% said 'wrong track'. This was a marginal improvement on the 2008 figures. But whereas in 2008 the 'wrong trackers' split 62–36 for the Democrats, in 2010 they split 75–23 for the Republicans, an enormous reversal for the Democrats.

Ask about the role of and their level of satisfaction with the federal government, and there was more bad news for Democrats. Of the 23% who said they were enthusiastic or satisfied with the federal government, 83% voted Democrat. But of the 74% who said they were dissatisfied or angry with the federal government, 65% voted Republican — and of the 26% who said they were angry, 84% voted Republican.

Finally, of great significance were the views of independent voters regarding the president, right track/wrong track, and the role of the federal government. Independent voters split 35–60 when it came to approval/disapproval of the way Barack Obama is handling his job as president (see Figure 1.1); they split 14–79 when it came to right track/wrong track (see Figure 1.2); and they split 34–60 when it came to the question of whether the federal government should do more or was doing too much (see Figure 1.3). This was a significant turnabout from 2008 when they had given the majority of their votes to Obama.

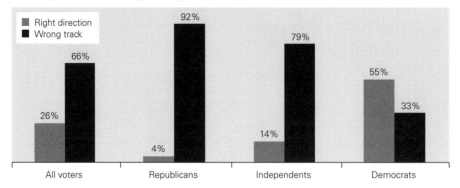

Figure 1.2 Do you think that things in this country are going in the right direction, or do you feel that things have gone pretty seriously off on the wrong track?

Source: Resurgent Republic–Democracy Corps Post-election Survey, 2–3 November 2010

Figure 1.3 Opinions on the role of federal government, November 2010

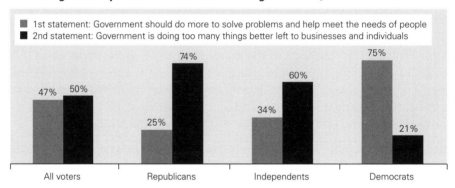

Source: Resurgent Republic–Democracy Corps Post-election Survey, 2–3 November 2010

Conclusion

Following these elections, one can drive from the Pacific coast to the Atlantic coast — 4,800 kilometres — and not travel through a single congressional district held by a Democrat. Large swathes of middle America have again been engulfed by Republican red on the electoral map. The Democrats' blue is mainly on the coastal margins with isolated scatterings elsewhere. Republicans had their best showing among independent voters in congressional elections since 1994. Voters identifying as conservative were a larger share of the electorate (41%), and more voted for Republican candidates (84%), than in any election since 1976. Republicans gained 60% of the white vote, a level of support exceeded only twice in mid-term elections in the past 60 years.

It all sounds very good news for Republicans. But it's not all doom and gloom for the Democrats. As Bob Benenson pointed out, 'in terms of control-of-power levers in the federal government, the Democratic Party is still in a stronger position than it was 8 years ago', after the 2002 mid-terms. Back then, the Republicans controlled the presidency and both houses of Congress. Today, the Democrats still control the White House — and may do for another 6 years — as well as the Senate. The Republicans in Congress may yet falter and/or they may nominate a Tea Party mad hatter as their presidential candidate in 2012.

Questions

1 How many House and Senate members were defeated at the nomination stage (primaries etc.) in these elections? Give an example and explain why they lost.
2 Why did Senator Blanche Lincoln of Arkansas lose in the general election?
3 What common factor linked the Republicans' failure to win the Senate seats in Delaware, Colorado and Nevada?
4 What was extraordinary about Senator Lisa Murkowski's re-election in Alaska?
5 What does Table 1.4 tell us about the performance of the Democrats in the House elections in 2010?
6 Explain the term 'McCain-Democrats'. How well did they perform on Election Day?
7 How significant was House Democrats' vote on the Obama healthcare reform in determining their chances of re-election?
8 Summarise what Table 1.5 tells us about the Democrats' performance in 2010.
9 Analyse the significance of the data presented in Figures 1.1, 1.2 and 1.3.
10 Why does Bob Benenson claim that despite this poor performance 'the Democratic Party is still in a stronger position than it was 8 years ago'?

Chapter 2

The Obama presidency at mid-term

> 'His continued embarrassing on the job training implies the grim reality of him being a one-term president.' (*Houston Chronicle*)
>
> 'The statistical probability is that he will be another one-term president like Carter or Bush senior.' (*The Times*)
>
> 'He now looks not like a one-term president but a half-term president.' (*Sky News*)

As Chapter 1 has explained, President Obama suffered a historic reversal in the 2010 mid-term congressional elections. His Democratic Party lost 6 seats in the Senate and a staggering 63 in the House. The conclusions quoted above about the likelihood of a one-term presidency are therefore surely quite believable, or maybe not? For I have to come clean immediately: the quotations above were not made about President Obama in the weeks immediately after the 2010 mid-term elections, but about President Clinton immediately after his losses in the 1994 mid-terms. Clinton had just lost 8 seats in the Senate and 52 in the House. But, as we all know, Clinton bounced back to a comfortable re-election 2 years later. So the quotations above are offered as a cautionary note against jumping to conclusions following President Obama's recent reversals. Judging presidents at mid-term is a tricky business.

Job approval rating

In November 2010 — exactly 2 years after his initial election — President Obama's job approval rating stood at 47%. However, as Table 2.1 shows, a president's job approval rating at this stage in his presidency bears little correlation to his chances of re-election 2 years later. Whereas Reagan and Clinton — both with very low approval ratings at this stage — were both re-elected, George H. W. Bush, with an approval rating 15 percentage points higher than Reagan and Clinton, was not re-elected.

Obama began his presidency with job approval ratings in the mid-60% range. During his first year (2009), these fell to around 50% and in his second year (2010) they meandered between 45 and 50%. Figure 2.1 shows two interesting things about Obama's approval rating: first, that it fell in each of the first seven quarters of his presidency; second, that the biggest fall came early on — during the second quarter (May–July 2009), when it fell over nine percentage points in 3 months. Unlike most of his recent predecessors, Obama did not suffer a significant loss of approval during the second year of his presidency. So although historically Obama's approval rating at mid-term was low, this does not necessarily indicate that his chances of re-election in 2012 are poor.

Table 2.1 Job approval rating of presidents in November of second year of presidency

President	Month/Year	% approval	Won/Lost re-election
George W. Bush	11/2002	66	Won
George H. W. Bush	11/1990	58	Lost
Dwight Eisenhower	11/1954	57	Won
Richard Nixon	11/1970	56	Won
Jimmy Carter	11/1978	50	Lost
Barack Obama	**11/2010**	**47**	—
Ronald Reagan	11/1982	43	Won
Bill Clinton	11/1994	43	Won

Figure 2.1 Obama's job approval rating by quarter

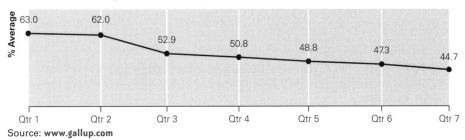

Source: www.gallup.com

Major achievements

Unlike his two immediate predecessors — Bill Clinton and George W. Bush — President Obama can legitimately claim some significant legislative achievements by mid-term (see Box 2.1). The first two items on this list might be regarded as easy to achieve: the first had been stalled by a Senate filibuster in 2008; the second had been vetoed by President Bush in 2007. But the other six items were all significant achievements for the president, especially the Patient Protection and Affordable Care Act, commonly known as the healthcare reform act (see Chapter 4).

Box 2.1 Major legislative achievements, 2009–10

- Lily Ledbetter Fair Pay Act (January 2009)
- S-CHIP Reauthorisation Act (February 2009)
- American Recovery and Reinvestment Act (February 2009)
- Patient Protection and Affordable Care Act (March 2010)
- Health Care and Education Reconciliation Act (March 2010)
- Wall Street Reform and Consumer Protection Act (July 2010)
- Unemployment Compensation Extension Act (July 2010)
- Small Business Jobs and Credit Act (September 2010)

The Obama team in the White House are proud that the president has fulfilled three of the five major promises that he laid out in his 'new foundation' speech at Georgetown University in April 2009 — healthcare, education reform and financial regulation.

Given this list of significant achievements, the president and his team might feel somewhat bemused that they seemed to get little or no credit for having passed this legislation. One might have thought that, as with President Johnson in the mid-1960s, such a list of legislative accomplishments would have resulted in the president gaining both credit and popular support, but not so. Indeed, when mid-term exit polls asked voters whether Obama's policies helped or hurt the country, 52% thought they hurt it — and 89% of those voted Republican. When it came to specific pieces of legislation that Obama had got Congress to pass, the reaction was much the same. Only a minority of voters approved of the economic stimulus package (43%) and the healthcare reform act (39%). Those figures fell respectively to 38% and 35% among independent voters. For Obama, this was achievement without approval.

But Obama's achievements were not limited to legislation. The Strategic Arms Reduction Treaty negotiated with Russia was another notable achievement — ratified by the Senate on 22 December by a 71–26 vote. Obama did much during these first 2 years to improve America's moral standing in the world and to improve international relations, especially among Muslim countries.

The president also made two widely acclaimed nominations to the US Supreme Court — Sonia Sotomayor in 2009 and Elena Kagan in 2010. There was none of the political fumbling seen in 2005 when President Bush tried — and failed — to get Harriet Miers onto the Court. Both Obama's nominees were widely regarded as strong candidates who were confirmed without major controversy.

However, there is a caveat here too. Neither nominee is likely to change the political balance of the Court. Both are liberals who replaced liberals. Although Obama was more fortunate than Bush to have two Court vacancies in his first 2 years — Bush had to wait until his fifth year for his first vacancy — Bush was able to move the Court in a more conservative direction by replacing 'swing' justice Sandra Day O'Connor with conservative justice Samuel Alito. Bush's Alito for O'Connor switch was a game-changing moment in a way that Obama's appointments have not been.

Relations with Congress

Obama made some impressive promises about how he would change the way things were done in Washington, and even change the tone of Washington politics (see Box 2.2). But promise has far exceeded performance. As Peter Baker commented in a *New York Times* article ('Education of a president', 12 October 2010):

Obama has learned that, for all his anti-Washington rhetoric, he has to play by Washington rules if he wants to win in Washington.

Box 2.2 What Obama said

'When we've made the changes we believe in, when more families can afford to see a doctor, when our children inherit a planet that's cleaner and safer, when the world sees America differently, and America sees itself as a nation less divided and more united, when we finally beat back the politics of fear and cynicism, and end the politics where we tear each other down — you'll be able to look back with pride and say that this was the moment when it all began.'

Victory speech following the Iowa caucuses, 3 January 2008

'We will be able to look back and tell our children that this was the moment when we began to provide care for the sick and jobs to the jobless; this was the moment when the rise of the oceans began to slow and our planet began to heal; this was the moment when we ended a war and secured our nation and restored our image as the last, best hope on earth.'

Speech after having secured the Democratic presidential nomination, 3 June 2008

'On this day, we gather because we have chosen hope over fear, unity of purpose over conflict and discord. On this day, we come to proclaim an end to the petty grievances and false promises, the recriminations and worn-out dogmas that for far too long have strangled our politics.'

Inaugural Address, 20 January 2009

In the same article, Baker quotes an Obama White House official as saying:

> It's not that we believed our own press or press releases, but there was definitely a sense at the beginning that we could really change Washington. 'Arrogance' isn't the right word, but we were overconfident.

Having Republican Congressman Joe Wilson shouting 'You lie!' at the president during his address to a Joint Session of Congress on healthcare reform back in September 2009 was hardly 'an end to the politics where we tear each other down'. Many of the debates about Obama's flagship policies have seen plenty of 'recriminations and worn-out dogmas' — on both sides of the aisle — as well as plenty of 'fear and cynicism'. Far from reducing the partisanship of Congress, if anything it seems to have continued to increase, and the tone between Democrats and Republicans has become ever more shrill. There's been little evidence of 'unity of purpose' and quite a bit of 'conflict and discord'.

Only one of Obama's five immediate Oval Office predecessors — George H. W. Bush — had ever served in Congress, and he served in the House of Representatives for only 4 years (1967–71), 20 years before becoming president. Carter, Reagan, Clinton and George W. Bush had never served in Congress. Obama was therefore the first president to come directly from Congress to the presidency since John Kennedy in 1961. But, like the first Bush, Obama had served only 4 years on Capitol Hill. Wishing to avoid the mistakes of his Democratic predecessors, Jimmy Carter and Bill Clinton, Obama recruited to senior positions in the White House staff people who had extensive experience as staff members in Congress. And as his White House chief of staff, Obama recruited Rahm Emanuel, a Democratic congressman from Illinois. Obama hoped thereby to build bridges between the White House and Congress to facilitate cooperation between the two branches of government.

But Obama failed to reach out effectively to Republicans in Congress. That said, the Republican congressional leadership was not exactly in the mood for bipartisanship. Handing over the writing of big ticket legislation — such as the economic stimulus package and healthcare reform — to the Democratic leadership in Congress also made bipartisanship unlikely. Table 2.2 shows how little bipartisanship there was in these first 2 years on Obama's flagship policies. With the exception of the reauthorisation of the State Child Health Insurance Program (S-CHIP), when 40 House Republicans and 9 Senate Republicans voted 'yes' on final passage, Obama's legislative agenda drew little in the way of Republican support. Indeed the healthcare reform bill drew none at all.

Table 2.2 Republicans voting 'yes' on final passage of Obama's flagship policies

Legislation	House Republicans voting 'yes'	Senate Republicans voting 'yes'
Lily Ledbetter Fair Pay Act	3	5
S-CHIP Reauthorisation Act	40	9
American Recovery and Reinvestment Act	0	3
Patient Protection and Affordable Care Act	0	0
Wall Street Reform and Consumer Protection Act	3	3
Unemployment Compensation Extension Act	31	2
Small Business Jobs and Credit Act	13	2

Modus operandi and personality

President Obama is in many ways very unlike both his two immediate predecessors — Bill Clinton and George W. Bush. In *The Promise: President Obama Year One* (Simon & Schuster 2010), Jonathan Alter describes Obama as the 'Un-Bubba president' — 'Bubba' being the southern term meaning 'good old boy' often used with reference to Bill Clinton.

Obama is certainly un-Clinton in terms of his political experience. Clinton came to the White House having had executive experience as governor of Arkansas for 12 years. Obama arrived with no executive experience at all — other than that of running a presidential campaign. During the Democratic primaries in 2008, Hillary Clinton ran a powerful negative television ad against Obama featuring a red phone ringing in the White House at three in the morning (see

Box 2.3). The ad worked because it played to concerns that Obama was too inexperienced in executive skills 'to lead in a dangerous world'.

Box 2.3   **The 3 a.m. phone ad (2008 Democratic primaries)**

It's 3 a.m. and your children are safe and asleep. But there's a phone in the White House and it's ringing. Something's happening in the world. Your vote will decide who answers that call. Whether it's someone who already knows the world's leaders, knows the military — someone tested and ready to lead in a dangerous world. It's 3 a.m. and your children are safe and asleep. Who do you want answering the phone?

Like Clinton, Obama is pragmatic, always well-informed and academically very bright. But unlike Clinton, Obama does not have a volcanic temper, does not preside over interminable meetings and is not chronically tired and late. Whereas Clinton was prone to self-pity and raging when things went wrong, Obama is merely focused on how to get things back on track. Clinton's sociability and talkative nature led him to allow meetings to overrun — sometimes by hours. There used to be a joke in Washington that during the Clinton presidency there were not four but five time zones in America — the usual four, plus Clinton Standard Time, which was usually hours behind everyone else's. Obama, in contrast, runs to time. 'Okay, guys, we have 20 minutes left. Here's what I want to do with the remaining time.' That's Obama's meeting style.

There are other differences of leadership style between Clinton and Obama. Obama is more disciplined, keeps his eye on the big picture, and is less easily distracted than Clinton was. Obama is much more of a 'process' person than Clinton — he believes better process makes for better decisions. He is also more of a delegator than Clinton and he does not revisit decisions once they have been made. Clinton was always second-guessing and revisiting decisions others thought he had already made. 'Clinton never met a rope line that he didn't want to work', commented Peter Baker in the *New York Times*. He always wanted to shake the hand of everyone waiting in line for him when he arrived at any event. Obama, on the other hand, 'does not relish glad-handing — that's what he has Vice President Joe Biden for', adds Baker. When Obama addressed a Business Roundtable meeting recently, he left straight after delivering his speech. He's not one for small talk and chitchat. Clinton would have stayed for hours.

But Obama is not only very un-Clinton, he's also in some ways very un-Bush. Bush's most significant leadership flaw was his incuriosity. Obama in a meeting will often ask, 'What am I missing here?' or 'Wait a minute, tell me more about that'. According to Alter, Obama 'believes in the power of poking, prodding and reasoning in a group'. This all sounds very commendable. But these 2 years have shown up some significant flaws in the way that Obama operates in the White House.

Presidential weaknesses and mistakes

The most notable and commented upon weakness which Obama has exhibited during the first 2 years is a lack of empathy. In this he is again quite the opposite of Bill Clinton. 'I feel your pain', was Clinton's famously empathetic line. He seemed to be able to put his arm around the nation and offer comfort and a sense of fellow-feeling. Obama too often comes across as aloof, detached and cold. 'Cool' is cool, but 'cold' is unattractive. As Americans suffer the effects of the economic recession, with unemployment close on 10%, the president has appeared above it all — unaffected and unfeeling. Here's how the outgoing Democratic governor of Tennessee, Phil Bredesen, put it recently:

> There doesn't seem to be anybody in the White House who's got any idea of what it's like to lie awake at night worried about money. They're smart. But they don't feel any of it, and I think people sense that.

Linked to this is another weakness — Obama's inability to talk in a way which most ordinary Americans both understand and resonate with. Too often he sounds professorial rather than paternal. George W. Bush might at times have had difficulty stringing together a coherent sentence, but he did speak in a way which ordinary Americans understood. 'I don't do sound bites', says Obama, which in one way is very admirable. But in another, it's rather naive, because ordinary folk understand and remember sound bites. 'Mr Gorbachev, tear down this wall', proclaimed President Reagan standing in front of the Brandenburg Gate in June 1987. Yes, President Obama has delivered philosophical lectures on race and religion, but does anyone actually remember what he said? The chattering classes are impressed, but ordinary Americans never really tune in.

It seems clear that the most significant misstep in the first 2 years was spending so much time and energy on healthcare reform. It wasn't a policy priority for voters in 2008; it still wasn't a policy priority for voters in 2010. Obama believed that he could get his healthcare reform legislation through Congress by the end of the summer of 2009, giving him a year to focus on the economy

---

Box 2.4 Obama's self-analysis

- 'We probably spent too much time trying to get the policy right and not enough getting the politics right.'
- 'There is probably a perverse pride in my administration — and I take responsibility for this — that we were going to do the right thing, even if short-term it was unpopular.'
- 'I make no apologies for having set high expectations for myself and the country because I think we can meet those expectations.'
- 'In a big, messy democracy like this, everything takes time. And we're not a culture that's built on patience.'

Source: extracts from Peter Baker, 'Education of a president', *New York Times*, 12 October 2010

before the 2010 mid-term elections. But as we know, the healthcare debate ran on until March 2010 — 14 months dedicated to it. Hardly surprising, therefore, that most Americans did not believe that he was focusing on the economy 'like a laser beam' — a favourite phrase of President Clinton's during his first 2 years in office.

What Obama needs to do

> Follow the Clinton post-1994 election model. Do what Bill Clinton did after his election losses in the mid-terms.

Matthew Dowd, writing recently in the *National Journal* ('It's not 1994', 20 November 2010), commented that he couldn't count the number of times he had heard this advice for President Obama in the days immediately after the 2010 mid-term elections: follow the Clinton model. Dowd continued:

> The Clinton model is to go back to the drawing board, manage the White House better, reach across the aisle and triangulate issues to get Republican votes in Congress, and communicate in a way that resonates more with middle America.

So here's what Clinton did and it worked; Obama just needs to do the same and it will work for him, too. It all sounds quite neat and very plausible. But hidden within this critique are two fundamental flaws.

First, 2010 is not 1994. Bill Clinton had entered office in January 1993 with unemployment in the United States standing at 7.3%. A year later it was down to 6.6% (see Figure 2.2) and in October 1994 — the last figure before the 1994 mid-terms — the figure was just 5.8%. Clinton had entered office promising to 'focus on the economy like a laser beam' and there was plenty of evidence 2 years later that his policies were working. Come 1996, Clinton's re-election year, with unemployment at just 5.2%, the economy was no longer an issue. Indeed, the exit polls in 1996 showed that 56% of voters thought the economy by then was 'excellent' or 'good' and those who thought that voted overwhelmingly for Clinton.

Figure 2.2 Unemployment trend, 1993

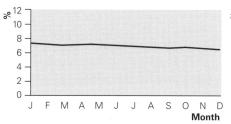

Figure 2.3 Unemployment trend, 2009

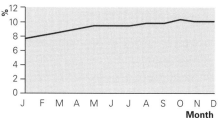

Source: www.davemanuel.com

Barack Obama entered office in January 2009 with unemployment at a level very similar to that of 1993 — 7.6%. But that's where the similarity ends. A year later, unemployment had risen to 9.7% (see Figure 2.3) and by November 2010 was at 9.8%. As we have seen, the 2010 exit poll data showed little evidence that people thought that Obama's economic policies were working. The president has argued that his policies have nonetheless prevented a much more serious economic meltdown, but that's rather like President Bush trying to claim the credit for preventing further terrorist attacks on the nation. Claiming credit for preventing something from happening is not the same as claiming credit for making something happen.

The situation in which Obama finds himself now is more like that of Reagan in 1982 than of Clinton in 1994. In October 1982, unemployment was 10.4% but Reagan managed to get it down to 7.4% by Election Day 1984 and he was re-elected. That's what Obama needs to do. Table 2.3 shows the high level of correlation between unemployment and presidential re-election. As Matthew Dowd comments:

> Although I don't disagree that Obama needs to govern more toward the [political] centre, the real problem with this advice is that it won't work unless the economic climate changes.

Table 2.3 Unemployment rate in month of re-election bid, 1976–2004

Month/year	President seeking re-election	Unemployment rate (%)	Won/lost
11/1976	Gerald Ford	7.8	Lost
11/1980	Jimmy Carter	7.5	Lost
11/1992	George H. W. Bush	7.4	Lost
11/1984	Ronald Reagan	7.2†	Won
11/1996	Bill Clinton	5.4	Won
11/2004	George W. Bush	5.4	Won

† But down from 10.8 in 11/1982

The second flaw with the Clinton–Obama parallel is that Clinton was a moderate southern Democrat who found it relatively easy to move to the political centre and do deals with the Republicans after the 1994 mid-terms debacle. But according to Professor Larry Sabato, 'Obama is an inflexible liberal who couldn't find the political centre with both hands, even if his career depended on it.'

As well as turn the economy around, Obama needs to do two further things between now and November 2012. The first is to get his presidential approval rating up from around 45%, where it's been stuck for the best part of a year, to over 50%. Table 2.4 shows that no president has been re-elected in modern times with an approval rating of below 50%.

Table 2.4 Presidential job approval rating in re-election year, 1956–2004

President	Year	% approval	Won/lost
Dwight Eisenhower	1956	68	Won
Ronald Reagan	1984	58	Won
Richard Nixon	1972	56	Won
Bill Clinton	1996	54	Won
George W. Bush	2004	53	Won
Gerald Ford	1976	45	Lost
George H. W. Bush	1992	37	Lost
Jimmy Carter	1980	37	Lost

The second thing Obama needs to do is to avoid a serious challenge from within his own party for the presidential nomination in 2012. Table 2.5 shows clearly that presidents who fail to do that — Johnson (1968), Ford (1976), Carter (1980) and Bush (1992) — go down to defeat.

Table 2.5 Intra-party challenges to incumbent presidents, 1964–2004

Year	President	Intra-party challenge?	Won/lost presidency
1964	Lyndon Johnson	No	Won
1968	**Lyndon Johnson**	**Yes**	Withdrew/party **lost**
1972	Richard Nixon	No	Won
1976	**Gerald Ford**	**Yes**	**Lost**
1980	**Jimmy Carter**	**Yes**	**Lost**
1984	Ronald Reagan	No	Won
1992	**George H. W. Bush**	**Yes**	**Lost**
1996	Bill Clinton	No	Won
2004	George W. Bush	No	Won

Of course, these factors — the state of the economy, presidential approval rating and intra-party challenges — are linked. Each affects the others. Obama has his work cut out in the coming 18 months — months which will decide whether he becomes a Carter or a Clinton. In January 2010 Obama, interviewed by ABC News' Diane Sawyer, said that he would rather be 'a really good one-term president than a mediocre two-term president.' Unfortunately, there's no such thing as a 'really good one-term president'.

Questions

1 What conclusions can one draw from the data presented in Table 2.1?
2 What have been Obama's most significant achievements thus far?
3 To what extent has Obama fulfilled the promises quoted in Box 2.2?
4 What does Table 2.2 tell us about partisanship in Congress during 2009–10?
5 In what ways is Obama unlike presidents Bill Clinton and George W. Bush?
6 What are Obama's most significant weaknesses?
7 What does Obama need to do to secure his re-election in 2012?

Chapter 3

Making sense of the healthcare reform debate

Do you remember *Jabberwocky* in Lewis Carroll's *Alice Through the Looking Glass*? It starts like this:

'Twas brillig, and the slithy toves
Did gyre and gimble in the wabe;
All mimsy were the borogoves,
And the mome raths outgrabe.

The trouble with trying to follow the debate about healthcare reform in the United States is that, like *Jabberwocky*, it seems to make no sense at all. Participants barely seem to be speaking in English: Hillarycare, single-payer system, Medicaid, Medicare, S-CHIP, deductibles, pre-existing conditions, public option, health insurance cooperatives, health insurance exchanges, individual mandate — the list goes on.

The first 14 months of the Obama presidency were dominated by the debate about healthcare reform. The debate reached its climax with a truly historic vote in the House of Representatives late on a Sunday evening in March 2010, when the House approved the Senate's healthcare bill by a vote of 219–212. This chapter will help you to understand the background to the complicated issue of healthcare reform in the USA, before we look at the story of its passage into law in more detail in Chapter 4.

Background

Unlike most developed countries, the USA has no universal healthcare system. Various presidents have tried to introduce one— notably Theodore Roosevelt (1901–09), Harry Truman (1945–53) and Bill Clinton (1993–2001) — but all failed to achieve their goal. During Bill Clinton's first term, First Lady Hillary Clinton was put in charge of healthcare reform. She came up with an extremely expensive and complicated federal government-run system — known to its critics as '**Hillarycare**' — but the plan got nowhere in Congress.

There is no equivalent in the USA of Britain's National Health Service — what Americans call a **single-payer system**. There are, however, programmes that cover certain groups within American society: **Medicaid** for the poor, pregnant women and people with certain disabilities; **Medicare** for the 65s and over; and **S-CHIP** (the State Children's Health Insurance Program) which provides coverage for children of parents who are fairly poor but not poor enough to qualify for Medicaid. If you're in one of those three groups, the federal government sees to and pays for your healthcare needs.

But what about everyone else — the vast majority of Americans? Their only option up to now has been to participate in one of the countless privately-run health insurance schemes. In other words, it is up to you as an individual to get health insurance, unless you just want to pay-as-you-go.

The problems

As the debate over healthcare provision started again in 2009, a number of problems faced the US healthcare system. The first concerned cost. The cost of healthcare provision has risen dramatically since the 1980s. As Figure 3.1 shows, the costs of healthcare in America have risen from around $0.25 trillion in 1980 to $2.25 trillion in 2007. In 2007, the federal government spent $754 billion on healthcare — over half of it on Medicare — and with America's population getting progressively older, that figure is set to rise in years to come.

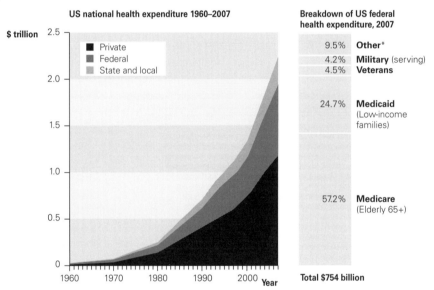

Source: US Department of Health and Human Services

Figure 3.1 Cost of US healthcare, 1960–2007

A second problem concerned the lack of universal cover. The US Census Bureau estimated that in 2008, 46.3 million Americans — around 17% of the population — had no healthcare insurance at all. This figure is open to debate: it may include illegal immigrants; it may also include people temporarily without health insurance because they are between jobs, as most Americans get health insurance through their employment.

This led to other cost-related problems. Because healthcare costs have escalated so dramatically, so have the premiums for the privately-run, employer-provided schemes. Indeed, it is estimated that they had doubled in the previous 10 years — a rise which is four times higher than the rise in wages over the same period. Private healthcare providers tried to compensate for this by increasing **deductibles** — what in the UK we would call an 'excess' on an insurance claim. In 2000, just 1% of US employees had an annual deductible greater than $1,000, but by 2008 that figure had risen to 18%. In other words, by 2008, almost one-fifth of insured Americans had to pay more than the first $1,000 of their healthcare bills in any one year.

Healthcare in the USA is so expensive that the $2.2 trillion that the nation was spending on healthcare in 2007 put it at the top of an international league table of countries' healthcare costs. As Figure 3.2 shows, whereas the UK was spending only just over 8% of its gross domestic product (GDP) on healthcare, the USA was spending nearly 16% — and the UK's 8% got its citizens universal coverage. This demonstrates that there is not a close correlation between money being spent on and the provision of healthcare — a point often lost in the healthcare debate in the UK.

A third problem with the US healthcare system was that even many Americans who did have some kind of private healthcare insurance were significantly

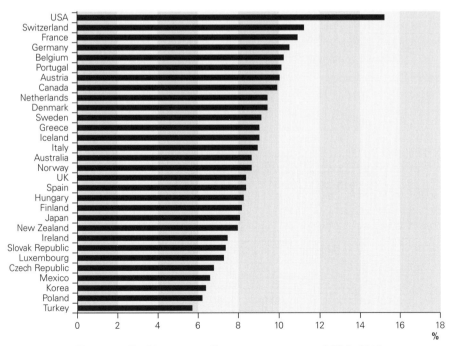

Figure 3.2 Healthcare spending as a percentage of GDP, 2008

Source: Organization for Economic Cooperation and Development, OECD Health Data, 2008 (Paris: OECD, 2008).

underinsured. Their cover was inadequate to meet their needs, so when these people fell ill, they had to make up the shortfall out of their personal income and savings. It has been estimated that half of all personal bankruptcies in the USA are at least partially the result of private medical expenses.

Fourth, there was the problem of **pre-existing conditions**: many health insurance companies would not insure you for a pre-existing health problem — an illness from which you already suffered when you tried to get insurance. The problem, therefore, was: get ill, and then you can't get insured. There was a further problem in that as many Americans get healthcare insurance through their employer. If you lose your job, you lose your health insurance; when you get a new job, you get new insurance — but not for pre-existing conditions.

Finally, the issue of healthcare reform also touches on the thorny issue of abortion. If the federal government becomes a provider of healthcare insurance, then it could be involved in providing abortion services. That position is not only completely unacceptable to most Republican politicians, but also to a good number of moderate and conservative Democrats, making it very difficult to get a majority to support it. But most Democrats — and most women voters — will not contemplate healthcare insurance reform that does not include the provision of coverage for abortion for those who want it.

Now you can see why so many presidents have failed to deliver healthcare reform except in small, incremental steps. This was the unpromising landscape that greeted President Obama when he decided to make healthcare reform the flagship policy of his first term. So the healthcare reform debate in 2009–10 was about trying to address a number of these problems, such as: cutting the long-term cost of healthcare; getting cover for most of that 17% of the population who still had no health insurance; making healthcare more affordable; and stopping insurance companies from refusing insurance to individuals because of pre-existing conditions.

The proposals

When President Clinton tried to introduce healthcare reform in 1993–94, he presented a plan — put together by his wife Hillary — and presented it as a fait accompli to Congress, for which strategy he was roundly criticised. So when President Obama tried to deliver healthcare reform, he outlined his own views in broad brush, but left Congress to draw up the legislation — the exact opposite of the Clinton strategy. The trouble with this strategy was that, devoid of much in the way of presidential leadership, the Democrat-controlled House and Senate went their separate ways. The more liberal House, led by Speaker Nancy Pelosi, went down the route of the **public option** — a federal  government-run healthcare system which would compete with private health insurance companies. The supporters of such a scheme — mainly on the left — suggested that not only would this provide the currently non-insured with the best option, but competition would help keep down the cost of healthcare. However, the public option was strongly opposed by the Republicans, so it would not be a bipartisan healthcare reform.

The Senate generally kept away from the public option, trying instead to bring some Republicans onboard with more modest reform proposals. Some moderate Senate Democrats were pushing another compromise proposal, the **health insurance cooperatives**, which also had some Republican support. Seen as a compromise between private health insurance schemes and the public option, the cooperative would not be government owned or run. It would receive an initial investment from the federal government, but from then on would be run as a not-for-profit organisation. Critics of the idea, including former Democratic National Committee chairman Howard Dean who is also a medical doctor, claim that these cooperatives would lack real clout to compete with the private health insurance companies.

President Obama came up with another proposal — that of a **health insurance exchange**, a kind of market place with different 'stalls' offering different health insurance plans. Obama believed that this would facilitate not only compliance with the new regulatory framework which the reforms would establish, but would also promote competitive pricing. In Obama's own words, the health insurance exchange would be 'a market where Americans can one-stop shop for a healthcare plan, compare benefits and prices, and choose the plan that's best for them'. It was this proposal that found its way into the law which Obama signed in March 2010.

President Obama also gave his support to the proposal that once healthcare reform was in place, all Americans should be forced to have health insurance — what is known as the **individual mandate**. This, too, became law in 2010.

The next chapter will take you through the historic story of healthcare reform as it unfolded between January 2009 and March 2010, and Box 4.2 will show you which of the proposals discussed here made it into the final legislation.

Questions

1 Explain the terms (a) Medicaid, (b) Medicare and (c) S-CHIP.
2 What were the five problems facing the US healthcare system before President Obama's reforms?
3 What does Figure 3.1 tell us about the cost of healthcare in the USA between 1960 and 2007?
4 What does Figure 3.2 tell us about spending on healthcare in the USA compared with other leading countries?
5 Explain the problem of pre-existing conditions.
6 Explain the terms (a) public option, (b) health insurance exchange and (c) individual mandate.

Chapter 4

Delivering change: the story of healthcare reform

What you need to know

- The background and terminology covered in Chapter 3.
- There were **three** pieces of legislation dealing with healthcare reform, only **two** of which became law:
  - the House bill (the Affordable Healthcare for America Bill) — not passed
  - the Senate bill (the Patient Protection and Affordable Care Bill) — passed
  - the reconciliation bill (the Healthcare Reconciliation Bill) — passed
- There were **seven** critical votes in Congress — four in the House and three in the Senate:
  - House vote on Affordable Healthcare for America Bill (7 November 2009)
  - Senate vote to end filibuster (21 December)
  - Senate vote on Patient Protection and Affordable Care Bill (24 December)
  - House vote on Patient Protection and Affordable Care Bill (21 March 2010)
  - House vote on Healthcare Reconciliation Bill (21 March)
  - Senate vote on Healthcare Reconciliation Bill (25 March)
  - House vote on Healthcare Reconciliation Bill as amended from the Senate (25 March)
- The president held a bill-signing ceremony to sign the Patient Protection and Affordable Care Act into law on 23 March.
- The president signed the Healthcare Reconciliation Act into law on 30 March.
- 'Reconciliation' is a legislative manoeuvre used to enable Congress to pass budget and tax-cutting measures more easily. It cannot be filibustered in the Senate.

Delivering his State of the Union Address to a joint session of Congress on 27 January 2010, President Barack Obama had this to say on the subject of healthcare reform:

> After nearly a century of trying, we are closer than ever to bringing more security to the lives of so many Americans… Here's what I ask of Congress. Don't walk away from reform. Not now. Not when we are so close. Let us find a way to come together and finish the job for the American people. Let's get it done.

Just 55 days later at a bill-signing ceremony in the East Room of the White House, the president signed the Patient Protection and Affordable Care Act into law. As he put down his pen to applause the president said simply: 'We're

done!' It was a historic and, at times, highly improbable legislative victory for the president — one which will define his presidency. This chapter charts the roller-coaster story of healthcare reform during Obama's first 14 months to the successful conclusion which had alluded so many of his predecessors.

Healthcare reform was clearly to be the flagship reform of Obama's first term. With the economy being by far the most important issue in the 2008 election, this focus was thought a touch foolhardy, but Obama had promised 'change' and passing healthcare reform would signal that change had finally arrived.

Congress gets to work

When President Clinton's healthcare reform failed in 1994, one of the major criticisms made of his handling of it was that the proposed legislation was drawn up at the White House by the First Lady, Hillary Clinton. Congress was then presented with a fait accompli. In his 1994 State of the Union Address, President Clinton virtually told Congress — 'approve this, or else':

> If you send me legislation that does not guarantee every American private health insurance that can never be taken away, you will force me to take this pen, veto the legislation, and we'll come right back here and start all over again.

The legislation failed to reach a vote in either house. Later, writing in his memoir *My Life*, Clinton admitted this tactic had been a mistake: 'Politics is about compromise', he admitted. President Obama was determined not to fall into the same trap.

So in the spring and early summer of 2009, all the activity of writing the healthcare legislation was on Capitol Hill, not at the White House. No fewer than five congressional committees — three in the House and two in the Senate — set about work on healthcare legislation. Rather than the First Lady being in charge, it was Madam Speaker — Nancy Pelosi — aided and abetted by Senate Majority Leader Harry Reid.

In mid-July, Speaker Pelosi unveiled a proposed healthcare reform bill that was an amalgam of the bills drawn up by the three House committees — Energy and Commerce, Education and Labor, as well as Oversight and Government Reform. It ran to over 1,000 pages. As usual, the Senate was working at a slower pace. On 23 July, Majority Leader Reid announced that the Senate would not be taking up healthcare reform legislation until after the summer recess. Although the news was not unexpected, it was a bitter blow to the president who had been pushing for some floor action in the Senate before the break. With Congress recessed for the summer and no definite proposals on the table, it was the opponents of healthcare reform who filled the vacuum over the summer months.

Growing opposition

July and August 2009 were not good months for the Obama White House. The honeymoon period was well and truly over and the president's approval ratings were starting to fall. A Gallup poll at the beginning of July gave the president a healthy 62% approval rating, with only 31% disapproving of the president's job performance. By late August, the same poll showed the president's approval rating down 12 percentage points to just 50% while his negatives were up to 43%. A 31-percentage point approval margin had dwindled to just 7 points in 7 weeks.

At the same time, public opposition to healthcare reform legislation — even before the specifics were really known — was growing. A Gallup poll in mid-August showed that more Americans would recommend their member of Congress to vote 'no' on healthcare reform than would recommend a 'yes' vote (see Figure 4.1). Nowhere was opposition to 'Obamacare', as its critics now called it, more clearly to be seen than in the raucous and rowdy town hall meetings held in districts across the country in August. Any member of Congress who dared to attempt a defence of healthcare reform was greeted with noisy heckling. The Tea Party movement (see Chapter 8) was now much in evidence.

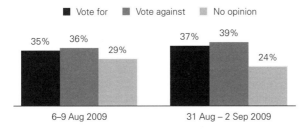

Figure 4.1 Would you advise your member of Congress to vote for or against a healthcare reform bill when they return to Washington in September, or do you not have an opinion?

Source **www.gallup.com**

The worst moment of this wretched summer for the Obama administration was the death of Senator Edward Kennedy of Massachusetts on 25 August. As a member — and lately as chairman — of the Senate Health, Education, Labor and Pensions Committee, Kennedy had worked tirelessly to promote issues associated with healthcare. Kennedy's Senate seat would be filled in the first instance by the former Democratic National Committee chairman Paul Kirk, on appointment by the governor of Massachusetts Deval Patrick. What no one could foresee at the time were the consequences that Kennedy's death would have for the chances of passing healthcare reform. For now, the president had more immediate problems with which to contend.

Retaking the initiative

By the time Congress returned to Washington after the Labor Day holiday at the beginning of September, the opponents of healthcare reform were firmly in the ascendancy. Polling showed that independent voters — one of Obama's key constituencies in his 2008 victory — now opposed healthcare reform by 2–1. The president decided to try to retake the initiative by the risky strategy of delivering a special address to a joint session of Congress — risky because if the president appealed for support and didn't get it, it would merely further damage his credibility and his ability to persuade. The speech was scheduled for primetime on the evening of 9 September.

In the speech, the president tried to answer what he saw as false criticisms of the proposed reforms. The White House-issued transcript of the speech contains this memorable moment:

> **President:** There are also those who claim that our reform efforts would insure illegal immigrants. This, too, is false. The reforms I'm proposing would not apply to those who are here illegally.
>
> **Audience member:** You lie! (Boos)
>
> **President:** It's not true.

The 'audience member' was Republican congressman Joe Wilson of South Carolina — a hitherto anonymous member of the House — whose gross incivility to the president was widely condemned. For his part, the president closed his address in suitably uplifting tones:

> I understand how difficult this healthcare debate has been. I know that many in this country are deeply sceptical that government is looking out for them. I understand that the politically safe move would be to kick the can further down the road. But that is not what the moment calls for. That's not what we came here to do. I still believe we can act when it's hard. I still believe we can replace acrimony with civility, and gridlock with progress. I still believe we can do great things and that here and now we will meet history's test.

And in the next 60 days, both the president and the Congress did just that.

'Change we can believe in'

Up to this point, the president had been criticised — even by some in his own party — for being too disengaged from the healthcare debate. 'It's hard to march if you don't have marching orders', commented Charles Jones, political science professor emeritus at the University of Wisconsin. 'If it's "We may go this way or we may go that way", it's hard to go back to the office and say, "We know what we're doing here",' added Professor Jones. From this point on, the president led from the front. The 7 days immediately following his address to Congress included a cabinet meeting, a meeting with a group of senators at the

White House, healthcare reform rallies in Minnesota and Maryland, as well as one-on-one meetings with senators Rockefeller (D–West Virginia), Wyden (D–Oregon) and Bennett (R–Utah) in the Oval Office.

The focus was now once more on the Senate, where on 13 October the Finance Committee reported out a healthcare bill by a vote of 14–9, with Republican Senator Olympia Snowe of Maine voting with the committee Democrats. 'When history calls, history calls', proclaimed Snowe, echoing the words of the president back in September. It was the first bit of bipartisanship we'd seen in the healthcare reform debate thus far.

By the end of October, the focus was back on the House, where on 29 October Speaker Pelosi introduced the **Affordable Healthcare for America Bill**. The now 1,990-page bill was immediately referred to seven different standing committees plus the House Rules Committee. Nine days later it was time for the first floor debate on healthcare reform in the House of Representatives. As the debate got under way, the president spent an hour on Capitol Hill making a last-minute personal appeal to House Democrats before returning to make a statement in the White House rose garden:

> This is our moment to deliver. I urge members of Congress to rise to this moment. Answer the call of history and vote yes for health insurance reform for America.

Abortion provision within the bill nearly scuppered it. Speaker Pelosi spent the day before the vote shuttling from meeting to meeting with different groups of House Democrats to get an agreement. First, she called together all her fellow female Democrats and told them: 'We're standing on the brink of doing something great. I'm not letting anything stand in the way of that.' Off she then went to meet with anti-abortion Democrats as well as lobbyists from Roman Catholic bishops. Then she went to another room where her pro-choice allies were closeted. She showed them her sheets tallying the likely votes: 'I don't have the final votes for passage', she told them, 'I don't know what to do.' In reality she did know what she had to do — accept tight abortion limits in the bill which she personally loathed. Back in the room with her female Democrats, there was fury. House Rules Committee chair Louise Slaughter, a leading liberal and close friend of Pelosi's, talked about 'all the women we were just throwing under the bus' and called it 'a betrayal of all the women that had fought for this for so long.'

Thus passage of the House's healthcare bill was finally secured only by an eleventh-hour deal between Speaker Pelosi and anti-abortion Democrats led by Congressman Bart Stupak of Michigan. In order to secure the votes of these conservative Democrats, Pelosi agreed to allow the Stupak Amendment to be inserted into the healthcare bill, thereby prohibiting the use of federal funds to provide abortions except in cases of rape, incest or situations in which the

mother's life was in danger. The amendment passed by 240 votes to 194, with 64 Democrats joining the 176 Republicans to secure its inclusion in the bill.

At just before midnight on 7 November, the House finally passed the Affordable Healthcare for America Act by 220–215. A total of 39 Democrats voted 'no' — mainly Democrats representing districts which Republican John McCain won in the 2008 presidential election — and just one Republican, Joseph Cao of Louisiana, voted 'yes'. This, however, was not the end, merely the end of the beginning, and much hard ground remained to be won. Yet this vote in itself meant that Obama had managed to move healthcare reform further than any president in almost half a century. It was at least a step towards that 'change we can believe in' of which Obama had spoken so often during the 2008 campaign. It wasn't exactly 'Yes we can!', but at least it was 'Yes we might'.

Back in the Senate

Eleven days after the vote in the House, Senate Majority Leader Harry Reid introduced the Senate's version of healthcare reform — the **Patient Protection and Affordable Care Bill**. With just 5 weeks to go to Christmas, the pressure was on for the chamber to move forward quickly — not a characteristic for which the Senate is well known. The particular difficulty facing the bill in the Senate was the need for a super-majority to get it past the inevitable Republican-led filibuster (where a senator or group of senators use the delaying tactic of 'talking a bill to death'). To cut off debate and end a filibuster, 60 votes are required — a three-fifths majority of the entire Senate. By good fortune, the Democrats held 60 seats (if one includes independents Joe Lieberman of Connecticut and Bernie Sanders of Vermont) in the 100-member chamber, but they would therefore need all their votes. There was no room for slippage. The Democrats had concerns about the votes of some of their more moderate members — people like Ben Nelson of Nebraska, Blanche Lincoln of Arkansas and Evan Bayh of Indiana.

The Obama White House was fully involved in the operation to persuade all those 60 Democrats to toe the line. In the forefront of the battle were Vice-President Joe Biden, White House Chief of Staff Rahm Emanuel, and Health and Human Services Secretary Kathleen Sebelius. In the week running up to the crucial floor votes, the president met the entire Senate Democratic caucus at the White House on 15 December. The first critical vote came 6 days later when at 1.00 a.m. on 21 December the Senate voted, on a 60–40 party line vote, to end the Republican filibuster of the bill. President Obama kept up the public pressure on would-be Senate waverers in his own party. The critical healthcare vote was scheduled for Christmas Eve — Thursday — so the president gave an interview to the *Washington Post* on the Tuesday, and to both National Public Radio and to Jim Lehrer on the PBS *News Hour* on the Wednesday. With a major snow storm bearing down on the capital, the

Senate convened at 7.00 a.m. on Christmas Eve for the vote on its healthcare reform legislation. It passed 60–39, with Republican Jim Bunning of Kentucky not voting. All that remained in the New Year was for the two houses to sort out their differences and the bill would be signed into law — or so we thought.

Enter Senator Brown of Massachusetts

Following the death of Senator Edward Kennedy in August 2009, the governor of Massachusetts had appointed Paul Kirk as an interim senator pending a special election scheduled for mid-January 2010. For months, there was little interest in this election. After all, Massachusetts is one of the bluest of the blue states and had not elected a Republican to the Senate in nearly 40 years. In 2008, it gave Barack Obama 62% of the vote to 36% for John McCain. The Democrat's senatorial candidate for the special election, state Attorney General Martha Coakley, began the campaign with a 30 percentage point lead over her Republican rival, a little-known state senator, Scott Brown. But the combination of a lacklustre campaign from Coakley and a populist, anti-Washington, anti-healthcare reform campaign from Brown propelled the Republican into the lead in the final week's polls. In one of the biggest upsets in recent Senate electoral history, Brown defeated Coakley by 5 percentage points — 52 to 47.

This was a bitter irony for the Democrats: they had lost the Senate seat held for almost 50 years by the champion of healthcare reform and in so doing had lost their critical sixtieth vote in the Senate, meaning that they could no longer break a Republican filibuster with a party line vote. Thus, they had significantly reduced the chances of passing their flagship reform. The likely scenario now appeared to be: the House and Senate had passed different versions of the healthcare reform bill; the compromise version yet to be worked out between the two chambers would have to be voted on again by both houses; the Republicans would mount a filibuster in the Senate; with only 59 votes the Democrats would be unable to break it. Healthcare reform would be lost.

Shortly after 6.00 p.m. on 19 January — just hours before the polls closed in Massachusetts — President Obama summoned House Speaker Pelosi and Senate Majority Leader Reid to the Oval Office to discuss the impending calamity. He didn't even wait for the votes to be counted. What were they going to do now about healthcare reform? Senate leader Reid had a solution — simply get the House to pass the Senate version of the bill and then send it to the president for his signature. But Speaker Pelosi was having none of it. 'The Senate bill is a non-starter', she said. 'I can't sell that to my members.' According to *Washington Post* reporter Ceci Connolly ('How Obama revived his healthcare bill', 23 March 2010):

> Pelosi lectured the others about the political realities of the House: her Democratic troops did not trust the Senate and she would face a mutiny if she asked them to do what Reid was suggesting. They talked round and round, repeating the arguments Obama had heard for weeks. This was not

how the president had envisioned things. He was just one day away from celebrating his first year in office. By now, he was to have signed into law a landmark bill guaranteeing healthcare to every American, the broadest piece of social policy legislation since President Lyndon Johnson's Great Society. Instead he was confronting the very real prospect of failure on an equally grand scale. There went healthcare reform. There went history.

As Pelosi and Reid left the White House that evening, the major participants in the push for healthcare reform were beginning to think that they had made some strategic mistakes from which they might not recover: tackling healthcare at all in the teeth of a recession; their subsequent failure to focus sufficiently on the economy and jobs; the White House's surrender of control on healthcare to the Democratic leadership in Congress. And so the strategy changed — the president was now going to be back in charge with Pelosi and Reid there to deliver the votes. White House communications director Dan Pfeiffer put it this way in a staff meeting: 'In 2010, the president has to look like he is leading the process.'

Obama as persuader-in-chief

During his 2008 election campaign, Obama had promised to change the way legislative business was done in Washington, specifically to bring legislative deal-making out of closed door meetings. The president now felt vulnerable from critics of the backroom wheeling and dealing which had characterised the healthcare debate thus far. So when his chief of staff Rahm Emanuel suggested holding public meetings with congressional Republicans, Obama quickly embraced the idea. Two days after his State of the Union Address to a joint session of Congress, the president headed to Baltimore, Maryland, to address the Republican House Issues Conference being held that weekend.

The Republicans wanted to scale down the reform package, but the president wasn't interested. At a meeting back at the White House, the president ridiculed the House Republican leader John Boehner's proposal to scale down reform. 'Covering [only] 3 million people is not our goal', he reminded his staff in a Roosevelt Room meeting. That's not to say there weren't people in the White House who thought it would be prudent if the president did scale back his grandiose plans. Emanuel had seen the Clinton administration fail with its grand scheme in 1993–94 only to come back later with some smaller, incremental changes. 'Better to get points on the scoreboard' with modest successes than to have nothing, he remarked to the president.

After seeing their candidate defeated in Massachusetts of all places, many Democrats feared annihilation in the mid-terms in November if they voted for what was still an unpopular proposal. But the president was pressing ahead, publishing new healthcare proposals in late-February as well as holding yet another bipartisan event, this time at Blair House opposite the White

House. Even as the president was reaching out to individual Republicans — Peter Roskam of Illinois, John Shadegg of Arizona and Tom Coburn of Oklahoma — the Republican leadership was calling the president's efforts an eleventh-hour publicity stunt. They would not be voting for Obamacare. But the president had made it clear after the Blair House summit that the time for debate was over. He would move ahead with healthcare reform with or without Republican support.

The president took his message outside Washington (see Box 4.1) — to town hall meetings in Tampa, Florida (28 January), Nashua, New Hampshire (2 February), Willow Grove, Pennsylvania (8 March), St Louis, Missouri (10 March), Strongsville, Ohio (15 March) and Fairfax, Virginia (19 March). March also saw Obama at a White House event, surrounded by doctors in white medical coats, calling for an up or down vote in Congress.

Box 4.1	Timeline of President Obama's healthcare involvement, 27 January – 20 March 2010
27 January	Delivers State of the Union Address to Congress: 'don't walk away from [healthcare] reform...let's get it done'
28 January	Addresses town hall meeting, Tampa, Florida
29 January	Addresses Republican House Issues Conference, Baltimore, Maryland
2 February	Addresses town hall meeting, Nashua, New Hampshire
3 February	Takes part in televised session with Senate Democrats, Newseum, Washington DC
6 February	Addresses Democratic National Committee Winter Meeting, Capitol Hilton, Washington DC
22 February	Publishes new healthcare reform proposals
25 February	Hosts bipartisan healthcare reform meeting, Blair House, Washington DC
3 March	Calls for 'up or down' vote on healthcare reform in Congress at White House East Room event
4 March	Meets 11 House Democrats, Roosevelt Room Meets New Democratic Coalition Leadership, Oval Office Meets Senator Schumer (D-NY), Oval Office
8 March	Attends healthcare reform event, Willow Grove, Pennsylvania
10 March	Attends healthcare reform event, St Louis, Missouri
12 March	White House press secretary announces 3-day delay in president's trip to Indonesia, Guam and Australia (from 18 to 21 March) so that he can urge passage of healthcare reform legislation (later postponed to June)
15 March	Addresses town hall meeting, Strongsville, Ohio
18 March	Reconciliation Bill published: debate in House set for 1.00 p.m. on 21 March
19 March	Addresses healthcare reform rally, George Mason University, Fairfax, Virginia
20 March	Addresses House Democratic caucus, Capitol Hill

The White House now had a strategy to get round a Republican filibuster in the Senate — drawn up by Chief of Staff Emanuel and his deputy Jim Messina. First, the House would adopt the Senate bill. Second, the House would approve a batch of amendments in a separate budget 'reconciliation' bill. Third, the Senate would approve the reconciliation bill containing the amendments — but because it was a reconciliation bill, and reconciliation bills can't be filibustered, it would need only 51 votes to pass, not 60. As the Democrats still had 59 votes in the Senate this was feasible. On Thursday 18 March the **Healthcare Reconciliation Bill** was published and the debate and votes in the House on both bills was set for Sunday 21 March. The president cancelled a planned trip to Indonesia and Australia to lobby for votes. In that final week up to the House vote on the Sunday evening, the president spoke to 92 lawmakers either in person or by phone. In addition to that, on the final Saturday he went to Capitol Hill to address the entire House Democratic caucus.

'This is what change looks like'

On the afternoon of Sunday 21 March, the House began its debate on the Senate's Patient Protection and Affordable Care Bill. With 431 members available to vote — there were at the time four vacant seats caused by death and resignations — 216 votes were needed if all members voted. After almost 10 hours of debate, at 10.44 p.m., there were cheers and chants of 'Yes we can!' from Democrats as the magic figure of 216 was reached. The final vote tally was 219–212, with 34 Democrats joining the 178 Republicans in voting 'no'. An hour later, the Healthcare Reconciliation Bill passed 220–211.

Despite the lateness of the hour and the length of time this had taken — over 14 months — there were celebrations at both ends of Pennsylvania Avenue. At a quarter-to-midnight, the president appeared in front of the cameras in an otherwise deserted East Room at the White House to proclaim that 'this is what change looks like'. At just past midnight, Speaker Nancy Pelosi and other members of the Democratic leadership held a press conference in the Capitol. It was a truly historic moment — a victory that at times had looked highly unlikely. The president and congressional Democrats had achieved what many Washington insiders, Republican critics and professional nay-sayers had said they wouldn't and couldn't do.

Box 4.2   Major provisions of the Healthcare Reconciliation Act 2010

- **Coverage:** 95% of legal residents under 65 (compared with 83% before reform)
- **Costs:** $940 billion over 10 years
- **Federal budget deficits:** estimated to be reduced by $138 billion
- **Paid for by:** new tax on high-premium ('Cadillac') plans from 2018; increased Medicare tax on capital gains, dividends, interest and other 'unearned income'; fees on insurance companies, medical device and drug manufacturers; tax on individuals without coverage; cuts in Medicare

- **Individuals' requirement:** all US citizens and legal residents to have coverage; penalty of up to 2.5% of income for failure to get coverage; some exemptions (including illegal immigrants)
- **Employers' requirement:** employers of 50 or more full-time workers who do not offer coverage to pay a fee of $2,000 per worker; help for mid-size businesses by exempting first 30 workers in fee calculation
- **New provision:** no public option, but Office of Personnel Management to set up new low-cost national health plan to be run by private non-profit companies and available through new national health exchanges created by the Act
- **Pre-existing conditions:** from 2014, insurers barred from denying coverage to adults with pre-existing conditions; adults previously refused health insurance because of pre-existing conditions can sign up for high risk insurance until 2014; from 2010, insurers barred from denying coverage to children with pre-existing conditions
- **Children:** allowed to remain on parents' health coverage until age 26
- **Abortion services:** strict limits imposed to prevent federal funds being used for abortion services; exceptions made for cases of rape, incest and danger to the life of the mother
- **Illegal immigrants:** to be barred from receiving government subsidies or using their own money to buy coverage offered by private companies in the new national health exchanges

The House vote analysed

The data in Table 4.1 on p. 42 help us to analyse those 34 Democrats who voted 'no' on the passage of the Patient Protection and Affordable Care Bill in the House that Sunday evening. What motivated 34 members of the president's own party to vote against his flagship policy? Who were they? What did they have in common?

The second column in Table 4.1 shows that 17 (50%) came from the South while a further 9 (26%) came from states in an ark from Illinois to the northeast coast. Only 5 (14%) came from states lying west of the Mississippi outside of the South — Stephanie Herseth Sandlin (South Dakota), Jim Matheson (Utah), Walt Minnick (Idaho), Ike Skelton (Missouri) and Harry Teague (New Mexico). In column 3 we can see that 13 (38%) were elected to the House in either 2006 or 2008 while only 3 (9%) had served in the House for more than ten full terms — John Tanner (11th term), Rick Boucher (14th term) and Ike Skelton (17th term).

Perhaps the most surprising feature of this analysis are the data in column 4. In the 2008 House elections, 61 members were elected with less than 55% of the vote — generally regarded as the benchmark for a competitive district. Of those 61, just 25 were Democrats. By March 2010, Eric Massa (New York) had resigned and Parker Griffith (Alabama) had switched parties to join the Republicans, leaving 23 House Democrats representing

Table 4.1 House Democrats voting 'no' on healthcare reform, March 2010

Member	District	First elected	2008 % vote	Blue Dog	Conservative	McCain-Democrat
John Adler	New Jersey 3rd	2008	52		✓ (36)	
Jason Altmire	Pennsylvania 4th	2006	56	✓	✓ (18)	✓
Mike Arcuri	New York 24th	2006	51	✓	✓ (33)	
John Barrow	Georgia 12th	2004	66	✓	✓ (23)	
Marion Berry	Arkansas 1st	1996	Unopposed	✓		✓
Dan Boren	Oklahoma 2nd	2004	70	✓	✓ (5)	✓
Rick Boucher	Virginia 9th	1982	Unopposed			✓
Bobby Bright	Alabama 2nd	2008	50	✓	✓ (1)	✓
Ben Chandler	Kentucky 6th	2004	65	✓		✓
Travis Childers	Mississippi 1st	2008	54	✓	✓ (3)	✓
Artur Davis	Alabama 7th	2002	Unopposed		✓ (28)	
Lincoln Davis	Tennessee 4th	2002	59	✓	✓ (11)	✓
Chet Edwards	Texas 17th	1990	53			✓
Stephanie Herseth Sandlin	South Dakota At-Large	2004	68	✓	✓ (21)	✓
Tim Holden	Pennsylvania 17th	1992	64	✓	✓ (30)	✓
Larry Kissell	North Carolina 8th	2008	55		✓ (39)	
Frank Kratovil	Maryland 1st	2008	49	✓	✓ (16)	✓
Daniel Lipinski	Illinois 3rd	2004	73		✓ (47)	
Stephen Lynch	Massachusetts 9th	2001	Unopposed			
Jim Marshall	Georgia 8th	2002	57	✓	✓ (4)	✓
Jim Matheson	Utah 2nd	2000	63	✓	✓ (25)	✓
Mike McIntyre	North Carolina 7th	1996	69	✓	✓ (6)	✓
Michael McMahon	New York 13th	2008	61		✓ (34)	✓
Charles Melancon	Louisiana 3rd	2004	Unopposed	✓	✓ (19)	✓
Walt Minnick	Idaho 1st	2008	51	✓	✓ (7)	✓
Glenn Nye	Virginia 2nd	2008	52	✓	✓ (13)	
Collin Peterson	Minnesota 7th	1990	72	✓	✓ (10)	✓
Mike Ross	Arkansas 4th	2000	86	✓	✓ (20)	✓
Heath Shuler	North Carolina 11th	2006	62	✓	✓ (14)	✓
Ike Skelton	Missouri 4th	1976	66		✓ (46)	✓
Zach Space	Ohio 18th	2006	60	✓	✓ (29)	✓
John Tanner	Tennessee 8th	1988	Unopposed	✓	✓ (32)	✓
Gene Taylor	Mississippi 4th	1989	75	✓	✓ (2)	✓
Harry Teague	New Mexico 2nd	2008	55		✓ (9)	✓

competitive districts. But of those 23, only 8 (34%) voted against healthcare reform. Six of these eight were serving their first term. Given that opinion polls were consistently finding the legislation to be unpopular with voters, one might have expected a higher proportion of vulnerable Democrats to be voting against it. The data published by Congressional Quarterly (**www.cqpolitics.com**) showing the 12 most vulnerable House Democrats 6 months prior to the mid-term elections reinforced this finding. Of those 12, only 5 (41%) voted 'no' on healthcare — Bright, Minnick, Childers, Kratovil and Teague.

From column 5 we can see that 24 (70%) of the 34 Democrat defectors were members of the Blue Dog Coalition. The Blue Dog website states that:

> As independent voices for fiscal responsibility and accountability, the Blue Dogs have a proven track record of offering bipartisan, commonsense solutions to some of the most pressing issues facing the United States.

In March 2010, there were 51 House Democrats who belonged to the Blue Dog Coalition, thus 47% (24/51) of them voted 'no'. The coalition takes its name from the long-time description of a party loyalist in the old days of the 'solid South' as being a 'yellow dog Democrat' — someone who would vote for a yellow dog if it appeared on the ballot as a Democrat. The term 'blue dog' was adopted because founding members back in 1995 believed that their moderate-to-conservative views had been 'choked blue' by their party in the years leading up to the 1994 mid-term elections.

Column 6 shows that 29 of the Democrat defectors were among the 50 most conservative Democrats in the House as measured by the *National Journal* vote ratings for 2009. These included 9 of the 10 most conservative House Democrats. Column 7 shows that 26 (76%) of the 34 Democrat defectors were McCain-Democrats — that is Democrat House members whose district voted for Republican John McCain in the 2008 presidential election.

Table 4.2 (p. 44) takes a closer look at the way all the McCain-Democrats voted. Of the 46 McCain-Democrats who remained in the House in March 2010, 20 of them voted 'yes' and 26 voted 'no'. But the 'yes' and 'no' votes correlated closely with the margin by which McCain won a particular district in 2008. Of the 15 House Democrats whose districts McCain won by more than 15 percentage points, 14 (93%) voted 'no'. The one House Democrat to defy the trend was Bart Gordon of Tennessee's 6th District, which McCain had won by 25 percentage points. Of the 15 House Democrats whose districts McCain won by only 5 percentage points or less, only 5 (33%) voted 'no'.

Thus the typical 'no' voting House Democrat was a recently-elected member from a southern or northeastern conservative and competitive district which had voted for McCain in 2008. Of the 34 'no' voters, only Stephen Lynch of Massachusetts did not really fit any of these characteristics. Lynch was first elected back in 2001, was elected unopposed in 2008, and is neither a conservative nor a Blue Dog Coalition member. John McCain gained only 38% of his district's vote in 2008 compared with 60% for Barack Obama. Lynch cast a 'no' vote because he felt the Senate bill upon which the House was voting did not go far enough in reform and was inferior to the

Table 4.2 Voting by McCain Democrats on healthcare reform, March 2010
(members who voted 'no' in bold)

Member	District	McCain margin (% points)	Vote
Gene Taylor	Mississippi 4th	36	N
Chet Edwards	Texas 17th	35	N
Dan Boren	Oklahoma 2nd	31	N
Lincoln Davis	Tennessee 4th	30	N
Bobby Bright	Alabama 2nd	26	N
Walt Minnick	Idaho 1st	25	N
Bart Gordon	Tennessee 6th	25	Y
Charlie Melancon	Louisiana 3rd	24	N
Travis Childers	Mississippi 1st	23	N
Ike Skelton	Missouri 4th	23	N
Marion Berry	Arkansas 1st	20	N
Mike Ross	Arkansas 4th	19	N
Rick Boucher	Virginia 9th	19	N
Frank Kratovil	Maryland 1st	18	N
Jim Matheson	Utah 2nd	18	N
Alan Mollohan	West Virginia 1st	15	Y
Jim Marshall	Georgia 8th	13	N
John Tanner	Tennessee 8th	13	N
Nick Rahall	West Virginia 3rd	13	Y
Ben Chandler	Kentucky 6th	12	N
Ann Kirkpatrick	Arizona 1st	10	Y
Vic Snyder	Arkansas 2nd	10	Y
Allen Boyd	Florida 2nd	10	Y
Jason Altmire	Pennsylvania 4th	10	N
Earl Pomeroy	North Dakota At-Large	9	Y
Zack Space	Ohio 18th	8	N
Christopher Carney	Pennsylvania 10th	8	Y
Stephanie Herseth Sandlin	South Dakota At-Large	8	N
John Spratt	South Carolina 5th	7	Y
Gabrielle Giffords	Arizona 8th	6	Y
Heath Shuler	North Carolina 11th	6	N
Harry Mitchell	Arizona 5th	5	Y
Mike McIntyre	North Carolina 7th	5	N
Brad Ellsworth	Indiana 8th	4	Y
John Salazar	Colorado 3rd	3	Y
Collin Peterson	Minnesota 7th	3	N
John Boccieri	Ohio 16th	3	Y
Charlie Wilson	Ohio 6th	3	Y
Tim Holden	Pennsylvania 17th	3	N
Suzanne Kosmas	Florida 24th	2	Y
Baron Hill	Indiana 9th	2	Y
Michael McMahon	New York 13th	2	N
Tom Perriello	Virginia 5th	2	Y
Betsy Markey	Colorado 4th	1	Y
Harry Teague	New Mexico 2nd	1	N
Kathy Dahlkemper	Pennsylvania 3th	<1	Y

House bill passed in November — which he had supported. Lynch was also the only House member to vote 'no' on the healthcare bill but 'yes' on the reconciliation bill.

| Box 4.3 | **What influenced the House Democrats who voted 'yes'?** |

- 186 (98%) of the 190 House Democrats from districts in which Obama received *more* votes than his national average (53%) voted 'yes'
- Only 33 (52%) of the 63 House Democrats from districts in which Obama received *fewer* votes than his national average (53%) voted 'yes'
- 118 (92%) of the 128 House Democrats in districts with *fewer* citizens aged 65 or over than the national average (12.6%) voted 'yes'
- Only 99 (79%) of the 125 House Democrats in districts with *more* citizens aged 65 or over than the national average (12.6%) voted 'yes'

'We're done!'

Two days later, the president assembled a goodly crowd at the White House for what must have been one of the most joyous bill-signing ceremonies in a long time. 'I think we have a happy room', remarked Vice-President Joe Biden when introducing an all-smiles President Obama. The East Room was packed to the doors with White House staffers, congressional Democrats and administration officials, as well as special guests such as the widow of the late Senator Kennedy. After delivering a rousing and celebratory speech, the president made his way to a table to sign the Patient Protection and Affordable Care Act into law, using 22 pens to sign his name. This is an old presidential tradition — President Johnson used 75 pens to sign the Civil Rights Act into law in 1964. The 22 pens were handed out to people who had played a special role in getting the legislation passed — principally members of the Democratic leadership in both houses and key committee chairmen.

That left just a few bits of tidying up to be done. The day after the bill signing, the president signed an Executive Order reaffirming that no federal funds would be used for abortion, thus fulfilling a pledge he made to conservative House Democrats in order to secure their vital votes. The Senate also got to work on the Reconciliation Bill, voting on the amendments tabled by the Republicans. This led to 41 back-to-back roll call votes in 13 hours stretching over 2 days of business with the Democrats winning every vote. Early afternoon on 25 March, the Senate finally got to vote on the Healthcare Reconciliation Bill and passed it by 56 votes to 43, with 40 Republicans being joined by 3 Democrats — Blanche Lincoln and Mark Pryor of Arkansas plus Ben Nelson of Nebraska — to vote 'no'. Republican Johnny Isakson of Georgia was hospitalised and did not vote. Because the Senate had been forced by the Parliamentarian to make two minor changes in the bill, it had to be sent back to the House for a further vote there. It passed the House 220–207 and was then sent to the president for his signature.

Table 4.3 Major votes on healthcare reform legislation

Date	Bill/vote	Chamber	Y–N	D	R
7 Nov 2009	Affordable Healthcare for America	House	220–215	219–39	1–176
21 Dec	To end Republican filibuster	Senate	60–40	60–0	0–40
24 Dec	Patient Protection and Affordable Care	Senate	60–39	60–0	0–39
21 March 2010	Patient Protection and Affordable Care	House	219–212	219–34	0–178
21 March	Healthcare Reconciliation	House	220–211	220–33	0–178
25 March	Healthcare Reconciliation (amended)	Senate	56–43	56–3	0–40
25 March	Healthcare Reconciliation (amended)	House	220–207	220–32	0–175

Good news? Bad news?

What will be the legacy of the passage of major healthcare reform for the Democrats in general and for President Obama in particular? It is hard to think of any president who has invested more time, energy and political capital in passing a piece of domestic legislation for well nigh 50 years — probably not since Lyndon Johnson's push for civil rights legislation in the mid-1960s. There were certainly many who thought that all this time and energy could — and should — have been better spent on jobs and the economy.

Polling immediately after the passage of the legislation provided mixed signals for Obama and the Democrats. In a *Washington Post* poll published just a few days after the bill-signing ceremony, 80% of respondents said that they viewed the passage of healthcare reform as 'a major change in the direction of the country' — precisely what Obama had campaigned to bring about (Figure 4.2). But of that 80%, only 48% thought that it was 'positive change' while 52% thought it was 'negative change'.

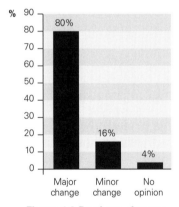

Figure 4.2 Do these changes to the healthcare system represent a major change in the direction of the country?

In answer to the question, 'Do you support or oppose the changes to the healthcare system?', 46% supported it but 50% opposed it. The same poll suggested that more people thought that healthcare would get worse as a result of this legislation rather than get better (Table 4.4), the federal budget deficit would increase (Figure 4.3) and the federal government would be playing too much of a role in the nation's healthcare system (Figure 4.4). Not exactly good news for the White House.

Table 4.4 Percentage of people who say the following will get better, remain the same or get worse in the long run as a result of changes in healthcare system

	Better	Same	Worse
The overall healthcare system in this country will be:	37	15	**44**
The quality of healthcare you receive will be:	18	35	**44**
If insured: your healthcare coverage will be:	17	38	**42**
If uninsured: your ability to get health insurance will be:	**48**	25	25

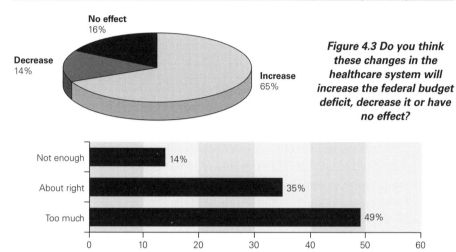

No effect
16%

Decrease
14%

Increase
65%

Figure 4.3 Do you think these changes in the healthcare system will increase the federal budget deficit, decrease it or have no effect?

Not enough — 14%
About right — 35%
Too much — 49%

Figure 4.4 Percentage of people who say the amount of government involvement in the nation's healthcare system will be too much, about right or not enough

However, the pundits brought good news for the president. 'Yes, they made history', proclaimed E. J. Dionne in the *Washington Post*, stating that 'the passage of healthcare reform provided the first piece of incontestable evidence that Washington has changed.' The conservative commentator David Brooks, writing in the *New York Times* ('The Democrats Rejoice', 23 March), congratulated both the president and speaker for possessing the necessary 'political tenaciousness'. He continued:

> Members of the Obama-Pelosi team have spent the past year on a wandering, tortuous quest — enduring the exasperating pettiness of small-minded members [of Congress], hostile public opinion, just criticism and gross misinformation, a swarm of cockeyed ideas and the erroneous predictions of people like me who thought the odds were against them. For sheer resilience, they deserve the honour of posterity.

But Brooks worried about the huge financial implications that this legislation will bring, and at a time of serious economic difficulty. As a consequence, said Brooks:

> This country is in the position of a free-spending family careening toward bankruptcy that at the last moment announced that it was giving a gigantic

new gift to charity. You admire the act of generosity, but you wish they had sold a few of the Mercedes to pay for it.

Conclusions

The passage of healthcare reform legislation is a historic achievement, no matter what view one takes of the long-term rights and wrongs of the policy itself. When most were advising President Obama and Speaker Pelosi to scale down their ambitions, they stuck to their guns. Both emerged with their political standing significantly enhanced. Back in the 2008 campaign, Obama had infuriated the Clintons — both Bill and Hillary — by remarking that:

> Ronald Reagan changed America in a way that Richard Nixon did not and in a way that Bill Clinton did not. He put us on a fundamentally different path.

Reagan had, according to Obama, changed the trajectory of America. Now here was Barack Obama as a transformative president, changing the trajectory of American politics. According to political commentator Mark Shields, this achievement marked the end — after 30 years — of the Reagan era. Ever since Reagan's arrival in Washington in January 1981, the agenda had been his — tax cuts and a scaled-back federal government. In the words of Bill Clinton in 1996, 'the era of big government [was] over.' To put it simply, this achievement said quite clearly that the era of big government was back.

Congressional Democrats also came out of this with a real sense of achievement. Whatever anyone calls it, the 111th Congress (2009–10) will never be described as the 'do-nothing Congress' — a frequent and often true description of many a recent congress. Speaker Pelosi emerged a hero, having proved to be the consummate legislator — showing skills of both leadership and compromise. I suspect that no male Democratic leader could have persuaded those female, liberal House Democrats to bite the bullet and support the compromise which was essential if final passage was to be assured. And remember, Nancy Pelosi gained a majority of votes approving healthcare legislation in the House not once, but four times — once on the House bill, once on the Senate and twice on the Reconciliation Bill.

How it will look in the long term is a more difficult judgement. It's like trying to judge the success of the Iraq operation the day that Saddam Hussein's statue was toppled in Baghdad. But at least in the short term, it showed the president's commitment to his policy priorities as well as his persuasive abilities. This really was — in the words of that much-used campaign slogan — 'change you can believe in'. Now he could rightly claim: 'Yes, we can!'

Questions

1 How did President Obama's approach to healthcare reform differ from that of President Clinton back in the 1990s?
2 Why was the summer of 2009 a difficult time for the supporters of healthcare reform?
3 How did President Obama try to retake the initiative on healthcare reform in September 2009?
4 What criticism had been made of the president up to this point?
5 Explain how the issue of abortion nearly led to the bill's defeat.
6 What was the Stupak Amendment?
7 Why was the election of Scott Brown to replace Ted Kennedy in the Senate in January 2010 so important?
8 What does Box 4.1 tell you about the president's involvement in getting Congress to pass healthcare reform?
9 What was the new three-point strategy devised by the White House to get around a Republican filibuster in the Senate?
10 What does Table 4.1 tell you about the 34 House Democrats who voted against healthcare reform?
11 What does Table 4.2 tell you about the way that so-called McCain Democrats in the House voted on healthcare reform?
12 What do the data in Figure 4.2 and Table 4.4 tell you about people's reaction to Obama's healthcare reform?

Chapter 5

The legacy of Justice John Paul Stevens

What you need to know

- The United States Supreme Court is made up of nine justices: one chief justice and eight associate justices.
- Nominations to the Court are made by the president, with the advice and consent of the Senate.
- Appointments to the Court are for life.
- For this reason, the president can make a nomination only upon the death or voluntary resignation of a member of the Court.
- In terms of judicial philosophy, justices may be thought of as being conservative, liberal or centrist.

On 9 April 2010, Associate Justice John Paul Stevens wrote the following brief letter of resignation to President Barack Obama:

> My dear Mr President:
>
> Having concluded that it would be in the best interests of the Court to have my successor appointed and confirmed well in advance of the commencement of the Court's next Term, I shall retire from regular active service as an Associate Justice effective the next day after the Court rises for the summer recess this year.
>
> Most respectfully yours,
>
> John Paul Stevens

Stevens was the second-longest serving justice in the history of the Supreme Court (see Table 5.1). His just over 34 years and 6 months has only ever been bettered by Justice William Douglas — the justice whom Stevens replaced. Douglas served on the Court for over 36 years. Stevens served under presidents Gerald Ford, Jimmy Carter, Ronald Reagan, George H. W. Bush, Bill Clinton, George W. Bush and Barack Obama as well as under chief justices Warren Earl Burger (to 1986), William Rehnquist (1986–2005) and, for the last 5 years, John Roberts. His distinctive presence will be missed on the Court, distinctive as much for his unfailing civility as for the bow ties he always wore. It has been a remarkable tenure that saw the passing of one judicial era and the arrival of another.

Table 5.1 The ten longest-serving Supreme Court justices

Justice	President who nominated	Year appointed	Year left	Length of service
William Douglas	Franklin Roosevelt	1939	1975	36 years 6 months 26 days
John Paul Stevens	**Gerald Ford**	**1975**	**2010**	**34 years 6 months 14 days**
Stephen Field	Abraham Lincoln	1863	1897	34 years 6 months 11 days
John Marshall	John Adams	1801	1835	34 years 5 months 2 days
Hugo Black	Franklin Roosevelt	1937	1971	34 years 29 days
John Marshall Harlan	Rutherford Hayes	1877	1911	33 years 10 months 4 days
William Brennan	Dwight Eisenhower	1957	1990	33 years 9 months 4 days
William Rehnquist	Richard Nixon	1971	2005	33 years 7 months 27 days
Joseph Story	James Madison	1811	1845	33 years 7 months 7 days
James Wayne	Andrew Jackson	1835	1867	32 years 5 months 21 days

A change of era

The Supreme Court that Justice Stevens joined in 1975 and the judicial climate of the day were quite different from those that prevailed when he left the Court in 2010. As Linda Greenhouse put it in a *New York Times* Op-Ed article ('One man, two courts', 11 April 2010), 'Justice Stevens entered the Court from one world, and he emerged from it in another'. How and why was this the case?

First, the Court that Stevens joined was distinctly liberal in its political and judicial philosophy, whereas the Court from which he emerged was distinctly conservative. The reason, however, for the Court's liberal leanings back in 1975 is somewhat surprising. Although by 1975 the Democrats had controlled the White House for 20 of the preceding 35 years under presidents Roosevelt, Truman, Kennedy and Johnson, only two nominees of those Democratic presidents remained on the Court. The other six members were nominees of Republican presidents, Dwight Eisenhower and Richard Nixon (see Table 5.2 on p. 52). Thus Stevens became the seventh Republican nominee on the Court, a fact which might lead one to believe that he was joining a conservative Court. But this was not the case as Table 5.2 also clearly shows. In broad brush terms, the Court consisted of three liberals and two conservatives, with the balance being made up of justices best described as either 'moderate', 'centrist' or 'maverick'. Indeed, even Chief Justice Burger's conservative credentials were far from reliable, making Rehnquist the only reliably conservative vote on the Court.

Table 5.2 Supreme Court membership 1975

Justice	Appointed by	Date of appointment	Judicial philosophy
William Brennan	Eisenhower (R)	1957	Liberal
Potter Stewart	Eisenhower (R)	1958	Centrist
Byron White	Kennedy (D)	1962	Maverick
Thurgood Marshall	Johnson (D)	1967	Liberal
Warren Burger	Nixon (R)	1969	Conservative
Harry Blackmun	Nixon (R)	1970	Liberal
Lewis Powell	Nixon (R)	1972	Moderate
William Rehnquist	Nixon (R)	1972	Conservative
John Paul Stevens	Ford (R)	1975	Centrist

Second, the political world in which Stevens joined the Court was still one in which the Senate tended to defer to the president in choosing Supreme Court justices. Unless they regarded the nominee as patently unqualified, and they might therefore be minded to reject him — and in those days it was 'him' — they tended to nod nominees through the confirmation process. Appearances before the Senate Judiciary Committee were relatively brief and unfailingly courteous, the debate on the Senate floor was perfunctory, while the vote was usually either by voice vote or, if recorded, near unanimous. Stevens was nominated by President Ford on 28 November 1975. The Senate approved his nomination by a vote of 98–0 on 17 December after a debate which lasted all of 5 minutes, from nomination to confirmation — 19 days. In 2010, it took 87 days for Stevens's replacement, Elena Kagan, to be confirmed.

Between the end of the Second World War and Stevens's nomination by President Ford, 22 sets of Senate Judiciary Committee confirmation hearings for Supreme Court nominees were staged. The average length of the resulting transcripts was 232 pages. For the eight nominations which followed Stevens's, the average length of the resulting transcripts was 1,845 pages. In 1975, just three interest groups participated in the Stevens hearings; in the eight nominations which followed, the average was 18, with 43 weighing in for the Clarence Thomas hearings in 1991. It is also significant that Stevens's confirmation hearings were the last ones not to be televised.

Third, Stevens was the last justice to be nominated to the Supreme Court in an era when the process was relatively non-politicised. Stevens was the first person to be nominated to the Supreme Court following the landmark judgement of *Roe* v *Wade*, which declared that women have a constitutionally-protected right to have an abortion. The decision had been handed down just over 2 years earlier in 1973, but the transcript of the Senate Judiciary Committee hearings shows that its members asked him not a single question about abortion rights. He had no record on the issue and not one senator knew what he thought about it. Five years later, the 1980 Republican platform called for the first time for 'a constitutional amendment to restore protection of the right to life for unborn children' as well as action by Congress 'to restrict the use of taxpayers' dollars for abortion'. The following year, 1981, Supreme Court nominee Sandra Day O'Connor was questioned at length about her anti-abortion credentials both by Reagan White House aides and Republican senators.

A change of thinking

John Paul Stevens joined the Court in 1975 having been appointed by a Republican president as a centrist or moderate conservative. Certainly Stevens's previous record as an appeal court judge was on the conservative side of judicial philosophy. Ford's Attorney General Edward Levi, in recommending Stevens to President Ford for the Supreme Court vacancy in 1975, wrote of him that 'he is generally a moderate conservative in his approach to judicial problems'. And Levi knew Stevens well. How, therefore, do we account for Stevens ending his tenure as the leader of the liberal bloc on the Court?

Some have suggested that this was because the Court Stevens joined in the 1970s was significantly more liberal than the one he served on from the mid-1980s, once the Reagan nominees O'Connor, Scalia and Kennedy had joined, and Rehnquist had replaced Burger as chief justice. This argument suggests that the so-called liberals of the Rehnquist and Roberts courts are just nowhere near as liberal as justices William Brennan, Harry Blackmun and Thurgood Marshall. Thus 'centrist Stevens' in 1975 becomes 'liberal Stevens' by the late 1980s. There is indeed some weight in this argument, but it is only half the story, and probably the less important half. The other half of the story is that Stevens himself changed: his judgements towards the end of his tenure were sometimes distinctly different — or even diametrically opposite — from those judgements he delivered earlier in his tenure. We can illustrate this with judgements in two areas — the death penalty and affirmative action.

Death penalty

When Stevens joined the Court in 1975, the hot-button topic was not abortion but the death penalty. In 1972, in *Furman* v *Georgia*, the Court had declared that the death penalty as then imposed was unconstitutional, as it violated the constitutional protection against 'cruel and unusual punishments' in the 8th Amendment. Following this decision, many states redrew their death penalty regulations, hoping that by so doing they would pass constitutional muster with the Court. The Court revisited the issue in the 1976 case of *Gregg* v *Georgia*. By a majority of 7–2, the Court reinstated the death penalty in the United States after a 4-year moratorium, and Stevens voted with the seven-member majority along with conservatives Warren Burger and William Rehnquist. Only Brennan and Marshall — both noted liberals — dissented.

But in *Kansas* v *Marsh* (2006), the Court — in a 5–4 decision — upheld the death penalty in the state of Kansas, and on this occasion Stevens was to be found in the dissenting minority along with liberal justices David Souter, Ruth Bader Ginsburg and Stephen Breyer. Two years later, in *Baze* v *Rees* (2008),

Justice Stevens went even further and announced in his separate concurring opinion that:

> I have…[reached] the conclusion that the imposition of the death penalty represents the pointless and needless extinction of life with only marginal contributions to any discernible social or public purposes. A penalty with such negligible returns to the State is patently a cruel and unusual punishment.

In this, Stevens was quoting verbatim from Justice Byron White's opinion in the 1972 *Furman* v *Georgia* case. After 33 years on the Court, Stevens had changed his thinking — he now believed that the death penalty itself was unconstitutional.

Affirmative action

Justice Stevens's thinking has undergone a similarly fundamental change in the matter of affirmative action and racial quotas. In his early years on the Court, Stevens was to be found in company with conservative justices on the matter. Three years after joining the Court, in *Regents of the University of California* v *Bakke* (1978), Stevens wrote an opinion along with conservatives Warren Burger and William Rehnquist, and joined by centrist Potter Stewart, which held that the racial quotas used by the university to deny a place to Bakke — who was white — while admitting applicants from racial minorities with inferior qualifications were unconstitutional. Two years later in *Fullilove* v *Klutznick* (1980), Stevens was in the dissenting minority again, agreeing with Rehnquist and Stewart. In this 6–3 decision, the Court's majority upheld a 1977 Act of Congress, which required that 10% of federal funds being spent on public works schemes should go to companies owned by those of a racial minority. Stevens disagreed, stating in his dissenting opinion that 'racial characteristics so seldom provide a relevant basis for disparate treatment', and that 'classifications based on race are *potentially harmful* to the entire body politic' (emphasis added). Indeed, Stevens appeared to go as far as to compare racial preferences in federal contracts with laws excluding Jews from citizenship in Nazi Germany.

But 15 years later — in *Adarand Constructors* v *Peña* (1995) — Stevens had changed his thinking. In *Adarand*, the Court struck down a federal government affirmative action programme on the employment of minority workers. Stevens disagreed with this decision and was one of the four-member dissenting minority, along with liberal justices Souter, Ginsburg and Breyer. When Justice Thomas, in his majority opinion, compared racial quotas with old-style segregation laws — because they both made judgements based on race — Stevens was enraged, protesting in his minority opinion:

> It is one thing to question the wisdom of affirmative action programmes… [but] it is another thing altogether to equate well-meaning and intelligent lawmakers and their constituents who have supported affirmative action over many years, with segregationists and bigots.

Was this the same Justice Stevens who had made comparisons with Nazi Germany back in 1980?

Often frustrated...

As the Court moved right and he moved left, Justice Stevens was increasingly left as 'Justice Dissent'. In his final 11 terms on the Court, Stevens was the justice most frequently in the minority in nine terms — every term except 2002–03 and 2003–04. While Stevens clearly relished his life on the Court, his dissenting opinions were increasingly seen to include a note of frustration — even annoyance — with his conservative colleagues.

Stevens will be remembered for his frustrated outburst in his dissent in the 2000 judgement of *Bush* v *Gore* — the decision which effectively decided that George W. Bush, rather than Al Gore, was the winner of that year's presidential election. In his dissenting opinion, Stevens commented acerbically:

> Although we may never know with complete certainty the identity of the winner of this year's presidential election, the identity of the loser is perfectly clear. It is the nation's confidence in the judge [guarding] the rule of law.

In his dissent in the 2007 cases of *Parents Involved in Community Schools Inc.* v *Seattle School District* and *Meredith* v *Jefferson County (Kentucky) Board of Education*, Stevens was again relegated to shouting from the side lines. Writing for the four-member liberal minority, Stevens claimed that 'it is my firm conviction that no member of the Court that I joined in 1975 would have agreed' with this decision. He made a similar point in his dissent to the 2010 landmark decision of *Citizens United* v *Federal Election Commission* during what would be Stevens's last term on the Court. Referring to previous Court decisions which the five-member conservative majority had just overturned, Stevens railed that 'the only relevant thing that has changed' since those earlier decisions 'is the composition of this Court.' Such incidents made ageing Justice Stevens look isolated, frustrated, almost an anachronism on the Court. But there had been times when Stevens was undoubtedly powerful and significant.

Box 5.1	**Extract from 'After 34 years, a plainspoken justice gets louder' by Adam Liptak, *New York Times*, 26 January 2010**

The Supreme Court announced its big campaign finance decision at 10 in the morning last Thursday. By 10.30 a.m., after Justice Anthony Kennedy had offered a brisk summary of the majority opinion and Justice John Paul Stevens laboured through a 20-minute rebuttal, a sort of twilight had settled over the courtroom. It seemed the Stevens era was ending. Justice Stevens, who will turn 90 in April, has given signals that he intends to retire at the end of this term, and his dissent on Thursday was shot through with disappointment, frustration and uncharacteristic sarcasm.

In Justice Stevens's early years on the Court, his views often seemed idiosyncratic, and he would often write separate opinions joined by no other justice. Over the years, though, he has emerged as a master tactician, and he came to use his seniority to great advantage. This term, though, Justice Stevens has been more of a loner. Thursday's decision, *Citizens United* v *Federal Election Commission*, was only the 10th signed decision of the term. In the previous nine, Justice Stevens wrote separately and only for himself three times. On a fourth occasion, he was joined only by Justice Kennedy.

A theme ran through these recent opinions: that the Court had lost touch with fundamental notions of fair play. In two of the cases, Stevens lashed out at the Court's failure to condemn what he called shoddy work by defence lawyers in death penalty cases. But the concluding sentence in [the *Citizens United* dissent] — what may be his last major dissent — could not have been clearer: 'While American democracy is imperfect, few outside the majority of this Court would have thought its flaws included a dearth of corporate money in politics.'

...but sometimes powerful

With the retirements of liberal justices William Brennan (1990), Thurgood Marshall (1991) and Harry Blackmun (1994), Stevens became the longest-serving member of the Court's liberal wing. This was highly significant because of the way the Court works in the assigning of who writes the majority opinion in any case. If the chief justice is in the majority, he gets to assign who writes the opinion, but if the chief justice is in the minority then it is the Court's senior justice among the majority who makes the assignment.

For all of Stevens's Supreme Court tenure, the chief justice has been on the conservative side of the Court — Warren Burger (until 1986), then William Rehnquist (1986–2005) followed by John Roberts. So, post-1994, whenever the Court split ideologically — the conservatives on one side and the liberals on the other — and the liberals were in the majority, it was Stevens who got to assign who would write the majority opinion. Craftily, Stevens frequently used this perk of seniority to lure swing justices Sandra Day O'Connor and/ or Anthony Kennedy to the liberals' side by offering them the authorship of the majority opinion. In an interview with Jeffrey Rosen in 2007, Stevens admitted:

> Sometimes, in all candour, if you think somebody might not be solid, it might be wiser to let that person write the opinion because after defending a position at length, people tend to become even more convinced than when they started.

For example, Stevens was effective in winning over Anthony Kennedy by asking him to write the majority opinion in *Lawrence* v *Texas*, the 2003 decision striking down sodomy laws. 'I don't know if I'm entitled to the credit or Tony's entitled to the credit, because he wrote an exceptional opinion', commented Stevens.

During his time on the Court, and especially in his later years, Stevens authored some highly significant opinions. In 1997, he wrote the unanimous decision of the Court in *William Jefferson Clinton* v *Paula Corbin Jones*, the judgement which led coincidentally to the discovery of President Clinton's relationship with Monica Lewinksy. Stevens was also the author of the 6–3 majority opinion in *Atkins* v *Virginia* (2002), which ruled that the execution of mentally retarded criminals was unconstitutional. He also authored two significant judgements concerning executive power during the administration of George W. Bush, both of which would limit the president's use of executive power — *Rasul* v *Bush* (2004) and *Hamdan* v *Rumsfeld* (2006).

'Learning on the job'

One's view of Justice Stevens's career depends on one's approach to judging and constitutional interpretation. Conservatives, strict constructionists, 'originalists' and most Republicans regard Stevens as, at best, a disappointment and at worst, just plain wrong; liberals, loose constructionists, 'living constitutionalists' and most Democrats regard Stevens as their hero.

About once a term, John Paul Stevens and conservative justice Antonin Scalia had a verbal set-to on a particular decision. In 2008, this occurred in the decision in *Baze* v *Rees*, in which the Court declared that execution by lethal injection was constitutional — it did not constitute a 'cruel and unusual punishment' forbidden by the 8th Amendment. In his dissenting opinion, Stevens showed how his 33 years of experience on the Court had changed his opinion on the death penalty. 'State-sanctioned killing is…becoming more and more anachronistic' he wrote, and proceeded to show that the supposed justifications for the death penalty — its deterrent effect and retribution — failed in practice. Stevens continued: '*I have relied on my own experience* in reaching the conclusion that the imposition of the death penalty represents the pointless and needless extinction of life' (emphasis added).

The phrase about 'my own experience' epitomised to Scalia all that was wrong with Stevens's judicial decision making. It enraged him to such an extent that he wrote his own opinion as a 'needed response' to Justice Stevens's separate opinion. In it he wrote:

> Purer expression cannot be found of the principle of rule by judicial fiat. In the face of Justice Stevens's experience, the experience of all others is, it appears, of little consequence. It is Justice Stevens's experience that reigns over all.

But this line from Stevens about 'experience' is quite revealing. It helps us to understand why Stevens has 'moved' during his 35 years on the Court. In a lecture at Fordham University Law School in New York in 2005, Justice Stevens offered another brief insight into the way he has approached his high court career. 'Learning on the job is essential to the process of judging', remarked Stevens. One cannot imagine Justice Scalia uttering such a remark, nor even approving of it, but according to *New York Times* legal columnist Linda Greenhouse:

> That modest sentence could be emblazoned on courthouse walls as the credo of the open-minded judge. John Paul Stevens never lost his willingness to test his instincts against his observations.

At a time when the judicial atmosphere — like the political atmosphere — has become more polarised than ever, maybe it would be no bad thing to have a few more like John Paul Stevens on the Supreme Court. Will Justice Stevens miss the Court? When interviewed in his Fort Lauderdale apartment by Jeffrey Toobin for a recent *New Yorker* article ('After Stevens', 22 March 2010), Stevens replied laconically: 'To be honest with you, I'd rather be in Florida than in Washington.'

Questions

1 How did Stevens's 34½ years on the Court compare with his predecessors' length of service?

2 In what ways does the chapter suggest that Stevens 'entered the Court from one world and emerged from it in another'?

3 Which two reasons does the chapter give for Stevens being regarded as a centrist or moderate conservative when he was appointed but a liberal by the time he retired?

4 What was significant about the length of time Stevens's confirmation to the Court took in 1975 compared to Elena Kagan's in 2010?

5 How had Stevens's views changed in the areas of (a) the death penalty and (b) affirmative action during his years on the Supreme Court?

6 What evidence is presented that Stevens became increasingly frustrated in his minority position on the Court during his later years?

7 How did Stevens use his seniority on the Court to enhance his influence on the writing of majority opinions?

8 Do you think Stevens was right or wrong to rely on his 'own experience' in reaching Supreme Court decisions? Explain your answer.

The Kagan nomination

What you need to know

- The United States Supreme Court is made up of nine justices: one chief justice and eight associate justices.
- Nominations to the Court are made by the president, with the advice and consent of the Senate.
- Appointments to the Court are for life.
- For this reason, the president can make a nomination only upon the death or voluntary resignation of a member of the Court.
- On average, appointments are made approximately every 2 years.

The vacancy

President George W. Bush (2001–09) waited over 4 years to make his first nomination to the United States Supreme Court. President Jimmy Carter (1977–81) never made one. But President Obama has been able to make two nominations to the Court within the first 16 months of his presidency. On 9 April 2010, Associate Justice John Paul Stevens wrote a brief letter to the president indicating his intention to retire from the Supreme Court at the end of its 2009–10 term. Appointed to the Court in 1975 by President Gerald Ford, Stevens had served just short of 35 years (see Chapter 5).

The nominee

Twelve days after Stevens announced his retirement President Obama met leading senators to discuss filling the vacancy. On 21 April, Senate Majority Leader Harry Reid, Minority Leader Mitch McConnell, Senate Judiciary Committee chairman Patrick Leahy and the committee's ranking Republican member Jeff Sessions met both the president and vice-president at the White House. The media reported that the president had already started informal discussions with potential nominees.

It was 3 weeks later, on 10 May, that President Obama announced that he was nominating Solicitor General Elena Kagan of New York to replace Justice Stevens. Aged 50, Kagan will become the youngest member of the current Court and its third woman — the first time in its history that the Court has included three female justices. Kagan joins Clinton appointee Ruth Bader Ginsburg as well as Obama's first appointee Sonia Sotomayor.

Chapter 6

Kagan's nomination set up a few other quirky 'firsts' for the Court. In terms of religious affiliation, this will be the first time that the Court has had no Protestant justice. There was a time when the Court was almost exclusively Protestant. Indeed, for much of the first two-thirds of the twentieth century, the Court contained what might be described as a token Catholic justice and a token Jewish justice. Thus, for example, during the 1960s, Justice William Brennan (1956–90) filled the Catholic seat while Arthur Goldberg (1962–65) and Abe Fortas (1965–69) filled the Jewish seat. As of October 2010, as a result of Elena Kagan — who is Jewish — replacing the lone Protestant, John Paul Stevens, the Court consists of six Catholics and three Jews.

Kagan becomes the 112th justice of the Supreme Court, but she is only the 41st to come to the Court without prior judicial experience, and the first since William Rehnquist was appointed to the Court by President Nixon in 1972. During much of the twentieth century, the appointment of justices to the Supreme Court who had no prior judicial experience was not unusual. Of the 42 justices who joined the Court between 1906 and 1972, 21 (50%) had no prior judicial experience, including the Governor of California Earl Warren (1953–69) and the president of the American Bar Association Lewis Powell (1972–87).

Unlike Sonia Sotomayor, Obama's first appointee, Kagan has no compelling 'rags to riches' life story to tell, having been born into a relatively prosperous, professional family. Her father was an attorney; her mother a teacher. Kagan's academic credentials were described by Kirk Victor in the *National Journal* ('Battle lines drawn', 15 May 2010) as 'eye-popping' — Princeton and Oxford universities followed by Harvard Law School. She later served as a clerk to liberal and civil rights icon Justice Thurgood Marshall, before going on to teach law at the University of Chicago and then at Harvard, where she became the first woman to serve as dean of the Law School. Between teaching posts, Kagan served in the White House Counsel office under President Clinton. In 2009, she was confirmed on a bipartisan vote (61–31) as the first female solicitor general.

The pre-match build-up

Some Supreme Court nominations have caused a great flurry of partisan bickering, even in the days before the hearings began in the Senate Judiciary Committee. The nominations of Clarence Thomas (1991), Harriet Miers (2005) and Samuel Alito (2005) come to mind. Pre-match bickering sometimes occurs because the nominee is regarded as either controversial (Thomas) or poorly qualified (Miers). It is more likely if the president's party is not the majority party in the Senate. It is often also a result of a nomination which may in some way change the ideological balance of the Court, hence the controversy over

Bush's nomination of conservative Samuel Alito to replace the more centrist Sandra Day O'Connor.

But, as with the Sotomayor nomination in 2009, none of these factors applied to Kagan. Kagan was regarded by most fair-minded people as well within the judicial mainstream, non-controversial and well qualified, and President Obama's Democrats held a 59–41 seat majority in the Senate. By nominating the philosophically liberal Kagan to replace the liberal Stevens, there was also no question of the nomination changing the ideological balance of the Court. If Obama had been filling the seat of conservative justice Antonin Scalia or swing justice Anthony Kennedy, then the feathers would probably have been flying, even if the president had nominated George Washington.

The Republicans' usual lines of attack were, therefore, somewhat closed off. First, they had to be careful not to be seen to be attacking a female nominee in a way that could appear ungentlemanly — all the more so as all seven Republican members of the Senate Judiciary Committee before which Kagan would appear were men. Second, Republicans might have tried to suggest that Kagan was unsuitable as a nominee because she lacked judicial experience, but the last Supreme Court justice to come to the Court without prior judicial experience was conservative icon William Rehnquist — who went on to become chief justice. Third, because she had no prior judicial experience, Kagan lacked a paper trail. Critics of a Supreme Court nominee find nothing easier than coming up with controversial judgements that the nominee has made while a judge in the lower courts. Republicans had tried this line of attack on Judge Sotomayor in 2009, but when it came to Kagan, this particular approach was also unusable. Fourth, Republicans might have hoped that the nominee lacked a certain winsomeness — that she might appear somewhat haughty, dull or lacking in humour. However, in Elena Kagan, President Obama had come up with a female — and liberal — version of Chief Justice John Roberts, who had charmed his way through the confirmation process in 2005 with quick-witted replies and a cracking sense of humour.

Finally, Republicans usually resort to attacking Democrat nominees to the Court as likely advocates and practitioners of 'judicial activism' — justices who will 'legislate from the bench', who will show little or no deference to precedent or to the laws passed by duly elected legislatures, whether in Washington DC or in the various states. However, in the year in which the conservative majority on the Supreme Court had in just one judgement (*Citizens United* v *Federal Election Commission*) 'reversed a century of law' — to quote President Obama — as well as overturned at least two Court decisions, this might not be a great line of argument either. Throw in a 'well qualified' rating for Kagan from the American Bar Association and an 18-seat Democrat majority in the Senate, and the Republicans realised that this was more coronation than confirmation.

The Senate's hearings

Elena Kagan's confirmation hearings opened in the Senate Judiciary Committee on Monday 28 June, exactly 7 weeks after her nomination. When Kagan entered the room on day 1 of the hearings, she found herself facing the 19-member Senate Judiciary Committee, composed of 12 Democrats and 7 Republicans — 17 men and 2 women — under the chairmanship of Democrat Patrick Leahy of Vermont. One might have thought that these events are called 'hearings' as it is a chance to hear the nominee speak for themselves, but what one actually hears is the sound of senators making long, rambling, prepared statements and taking an age to ask mostly predictable questions. To misquote Shakespeare, senators from the president's party come to praise the nominee; those from the opposition party come hoping to bury them. So on this occasion, for every compliment from a Democrat, there was an attack from a Republican. One struggled to realise that they were talking about the same person.

To Democrats, Kagan was 'unassailable', 'refreshing' and 'brilliant'; to Republicans she was 'a political lawyer', 'unqualified' and someone who 'seems to bemoan the demise of socialism'. To misquote Dickens, it was a tale of two Kagans — she was (pretty much) the best of nominees and (almost) the worst of nominees. When Kagan finally got to say something herself — that was late in the day — she promised, if confirmed, to show the 'even-handed-ness and impartiality' that the Constitution demands and proper deference to Congress and the laws it passes. She assured her audience:

> I will listen hard to every party before the Court and to each of my colleagues. I will work hard. And I will do my best to consider each case impartially, modestly, with commitment to principle and in accordance to law. The Supreme Court is a wondrous institution. But the time I spent in the other branches of government remind me that it must also be a modest one.

Nothing too controversial there. The nominee had safely negotiated the first day of the hearings.

Day 2 saw the beginning of direct questioning of the nominee by the committee. Whenever a senator asked her about how she might decide a hypothetical case, Kagan carefully deflected the question by saying that the issue was 'quite likely to get to the courts', or 'it wouldn't be appropriate for me to talk about that'. A somewhat frustrated Senator Arlen Specter of Pennsylvania, a Republican turned Democrat, repeatedly cut off Kagan, complaining on one occasion, 'I don't think I'm making too much progress.'

It may have been bland, but it certainly wasn't dull, enlivened as it was by Kagan's New York accent and wry sense of humour. Asked by Senator Specter if she thought the deliberations of the Supreme Court should be televised, she agreed with the suggestion before adding, 'It means I'd have to get my hair done more often!' Senator Kohl asked the nominee if she could 'tell us the names of a few current justices with whom you identify', craftily trying to elicit something about her judicial philosophy. 'I think it would be just a bad idea for me to talk about current justices', Kagan replied with a smile. 'My, oh my, oh my', marvelled the senator. At one point, Democrat Patrick Leahy got into something of a spat with Republican Orrin Hatch about the latter's line of questioning. Senator Hatch apologised to the nominee: 'We have to have a little back-and-forth every once in a while or this place would be boring as hell!' Kagan had an instant response: 'It gets the spotlight off me. So I'm all for it. Go right ahead!'

Day 3 found Kagan still at her canny best and Democrats more interested in criticising current members of the Court — notably Chief Justice John Roberts — than questioning the nominee. Indeed, at times Kagan was virtually cast in the role of defending her future colleagues, as Democrat liberals Ted Kaufman, Sheldon Whitehouse and Al Franken tore into the Court's controversial judgement in *Citizens United* v *FEC*.

Some days later, on Tuesday 20 July, the committee voted to recommend Kagan for appointment to the Supreme Court by a vote of 13 to 6. All 12 Democrats on the committee were joined by Republican senator Lindsey Graham of South Carolina in voting 'yes', while the remaining 6 Republicans voted 'no'.

Is there a better way?

A number of senators — on both sides of the aisle — appeared frustrated by Kagan's unwillingness to give detailed answers and to discuss her views on substantive issues. They found this all the more annoying given what Kagan had herself written about the judicial confirmation process back in 1995. Back then, while reviewing a book by Stephen Carter (*A Confirmation Mess*), Kagan had called for nominees to be more open in their testimony before the Senate Judiciary Committee:

> Open exploration of the nominee's substantive views enables senators and their constituents to engage in a focused discussion of constitutional values, to ascertain the values held by the nominee and to evaluate whether the nominee possesses the values that the Supreme Court most urgently requires.

In the same review, Kagan went on to praise the hearings in 1987 on Judge Robert Bork's nomination to the Supreme Court as they 'presented to the public a serious discussion of the meaning of the Constitution, the role of the Court and the views of the nominee.' (But in the end, Bork was rejected by the Senate.) She continued:

> Subsequent hearings have presented to the public a vapid and hollow charade. And what is worse even than the hearings themselves is a necessary condition of them: the evident belief of many senators that

serious, substantive inquiry of nominees is usually not only inessential, but illegitimate.

Many senators on the committee 15 years later were doubtless wishing that Kagan had heeded her own advice and allowed them to heed it too. In a *National Journal* article ('Is there a better way?', 3 July 2010), Kirk Victor saw it thus:

> Frustration over proceedings in which nominees have ducked and dodged questions and past instances in which nominees say one thing to senators and then act quite differently on the Court have convinced some observers that it is time to change certain aspects of the confirmation process. But if the process is broken, no consensus has emerged on how it might be fixed.

Some think that it's the television and klieg lights that are the problem. Geoffrey Stone, a law professor at the University of Chicago, certainly thinks so. According to Professor Stone:

> What's happened is that the hearing has become a kind of theatre, particularly with it being televised and the media focused on it. Everybody plays to the camera, and nobody really wants to watch anything but the candidate being grilled. The problem is that it is very hard for it to remain a serious process, given the fact that it has become kind of a circus because of the media. Almost nobody is playing for the actual question of, who is this candidate and do I think she should be confirmed? They are all playing for the TV screen and their constituents.

In the same article, Republican Senator Jon Kyl of Arizona, a member of the Judiciary Committee, agreed that most senators showboat for the cameras, but he doesn't see this is a major problem. He lays the problem at the door of the nominees:

> The problem is witnesses who are schooled to avoid saying anything controversial. If you really have a clever nominee, he or she can avoid giving away very much. And [Kagan], for example, is a very clever nominee.

During the hearings, senators repeatedly reminded Kagan of the article that she had written in 1995 criticising the confirmation hearings. But Kagan, now a nominee rather than an academic, saw things somewhat differently, and said that the article was 'a little bit off'. Some of today's academics suggest that a way of sharpening up the committee's questioning would be to have the lion's share of it done by well-trained lawyers brought in specifically for the task. Back in 1987, when Congress set up a joint select committee to investigate the Iran-Contra affair — a Reagan administration foreign policy scandal — most of the questioning was done not by senators but by trained lawyers. Some suggest that this is a model which could be followed for Supreme Court nomination hearings.

The Senate's vote

On 5 August 2010, the full Senate voted by 63 votes to 37 to confirm Kagan as the 112th justice of the Supreme Court. The vote came a year, almost to the day, after the one which had confirmed Sonia Sotomayor on 6 August 2009. The whole process, from nomination to confirmation, had taken 87 days — much longer than the average of around 60 days during the past 35 years. Table 6.1 shows that Kagan's confirmation was in fact the second longest during this period, beaten only by the 99 days it took the Senate to confirm the controversial Clarence Thomas back in 1991.

Table 6.1 Days from nomination to confirmation of Supreme Court justices: 1975–2010

Justice	Nominated by	Year	Days from nomination to confirmation
John Paul Stevens	Gerald Ford	1975	19
Sandra O'Connor	Ronald Reagan	1981	33
Antonin Scalia	Ronald Reagan	1986	85
Anthony Kennedy	Ronald Reagan	1988	65
David Souter	George H. W. Bush	1990	69
Clarence Thomas	George H. W. Bush	1991	99
Ruth Bader Ginsburg	Bill Clinton	1993	50
Stephen Breyer	Bill Clinton	1994	73
John Roberts	George W. Bush	2005	23
Samuel Alito	George W. Bush	2006	82
Sonia Sotomayor	Barack Obama	2009	66
Elena Kagan	Barack Obama	2010	87

The 63 'yes' votes were cast by 58 Democrats joined by 5 Republicans, while the remaining 36 Republicans and 1 Democrat — Senator Ben Nelson of Nebraska — voted 'no'. The five Republicans who voted yes — Susan Collins (Maine), Lindsey Graham (South Carolina), Judd Gregg (New Hampshire), Richard Lugar (Indiana) and Olympia Snowe (Maine) — were also among the nine Republicans who voted to confirm Justice Sonia Sotomayor, President Obama's first Supreme Court pick, in 2009. None of these five was to face their voters in the 2010 mid-terms — Gregg had already announced his retirement and the other four had either 2 or 4 years remaining of their 6-year terms.

Table 6.2 shows how partisanship in voting has increased in recent years regarding Supreme Court nominees. When the last Democrat president, Bill Clinton, nominated Ruth Bader Ginsburg and Stephen Breyer to the Supreme Court, they were supported respectively by 41 and 33 Republican senators. Contrast that with the number of Republicans who supported the two recent Obama nominees — 9 and 5 respectively for Sonia Sotomayor and Elena Kagan. Even when President George H. W. Bush replaced liberal justice Thurgood Marshall with arch conservative Clarence Thomas in 1991, 11 Democrats voted 'yes' on the Thomas nomination.

Table 6.2 'Yes' votes by opposition party senators on Supreme Court nominees, 1990–2010

Nominee	Date	President (party)	'Yes' votes by opposition party senators
David Souter	1990	Bush (R)	D: 46
Clarence Thomas	1991	Bush (R)	D: 11
Ruth Bader Ginsburg	1993	Clinton (D)	R: 41
Stephen Breyer	1994	Clinton (D)	R: 33
John Roberts	2005	Bush (R)	D: 22
Samuel Alito	2006	Bush (R)	D: 4
Sonia Sotomayor	2009	Obama (D)	R: 9
Elena Kagan	2010	Obama (D)	R: 5

Table 6.3 shows the professional background of Supreme Court justices since 1789. Eight of the nine current members of the Court were previously judges in the US appeals court. Elena Kagan — the only non-judge now on the Court — is one of 11 Supreme Court justices to be recruited from the US Department of Justice. Before Justice Kagan, the previous Justice Department official to be recruited to the Supreme Court was William Rehnquist, who was nominated to the Court by President Nixon in 1972 and then elevated to Chief Justice by President Reagan in 1986. Chief Justice Rehnquist died in office in 2005.

Table 6.3 Position held prior to Supreme Court appointment

Position	Number	Most recent justice	Date
Lawyer	24	Lewis Powell	1971
US Appeal Courts	21	Sonia Sotomayor	2009
US Justice Department	11	Elena Kagan	2010
State Supreme Court	11	William Brennan	1956
State trial/appeal courts	10	Sandra Day O'Connor	1981
US District Courts	9	Edward Sanford	1923
US executive branch (not Justice)	9	Arthur Goldberg	1962
US Senate	7	Harold Burton	1945
State governor	3	Earl Warren	1953
State legislature	2	Benjamin Curtis	1851
Law professor	2	Felix Frankfurter	1939
US House of Representatives	1	James Wayne	1835

Perhaps most significantly, Kagan's appointment to the Court means that for the first time in its history the Court now has three female justices, less than 30 years after President Reagan appointed the first female justice — Sandra Day O'Connor — in 1981.

The Kagan for Stevens switch

A question we often ask is whether or not a president can influence the political balance of the Supreme Court. (For a detailed discussion of this question see Anthony J. Bennett, *The US Supreme Court*, Philip Allan Updates, 2010, Chapter 2.) One of the important ingredients which must exist for a president to influence the balance of the Court is for the incoming justice to be of a different ideological persuasion from the outgoing justice. This is simply not the case in the Kagan for Stevens switch as both can be classified as judicial liberals. Kagan is unlikely to decide cases in any significantly different way from her predecessor. Indeed, as Stevens had become the most reliably liberal voice on the Court during the last decade, it may be that Justice Kagan's appointment might actually make the Court a little more conservative — not the direction in which you would expect a Democratic president to take the Court.

There is, however, another reason why the liberal influence on the Court may be weakened by the Kagan for Stevens switch. Since 1994, Stevens has been the most senior liberal member of the Court. During these 16 years, the chief justice was a conservative justice — William Rehnquist until 2005, followed by John Roberts. It is the custom of the Court that when the chief justice is not in the majority in any case, the most senior justice in the majority decides who will write the majority opinion. Hence, whenever Rehnquist or Roberts were in the minority, it was usually Stevens who decided who would write the majority opinion in a case. Stevens used this power to great effect, often inviting swing justice Anthony Kennedy to author the opinion in order to tie him in with the liberal wing of the Court. Four liberals (Stevens, Ginsburg, Breyer and Souter/Sotomayor) plus Kennedy meant that the four conservatives (Rehnquist/Roberts, Scalia, Thomas and Alito) were in the minority. Furthermore, Stevens's age, length of service and personal charm made him an adept persuader. Unlike some of his fellow justices, Stevens preferred to charm his colleagues rather than harangue them. Thus Stevens was able to magnify the influence of the liberal wing of the Court.

In the new Court that started in October 2010, the most senior justice by service is Antonin Scalia — like Chief Justice Roberts, a conservative. So he and the chief are unlikely to be on different sides of a case in a 5–4 ideological split. That means that the person who will inherit Stevens's mantle to award the authoring of opinions when the chief justice is in the minority is likely to be Justice Anthony Kennedy. Kennedy already has considerable clout on the Court by virtue of being the so-called swing justice — sometimes aligning with the Court's four conservatives, sometimes with the four liberals. 'Kennedy's clout could grow on high court', proclaimed the headline to a *Washington Post* article by Mark Sherman (11 July 2010). The article quoted Paul Clement, a former Bush administration solicitor general, as saying that putting the power to assign opinions in Kennedy's hands is the 'single most important dynamic change' brought about by Stevens's departure.

Questions

1 With whom did President Obama consult when he was deciding who to nominate to the Supreme Court to fill the vacancy created by Stevens's retirement?

2 What 'firsts' did Kagan's nomination create for the Court?

3 What was unusual about Kagan's professional background prior to her nomination to the Supreme Court?

4 Why did Republican senators find it hard to mount a significant challenge to Judge Kagan's nomination?

5 What qualities did Kagan use to see herself successfully through the confirmation hearings?

6 What had Kagan written about the confirmation process back in 1995? How did what she wrote then differ from her approach in 2010?

7 What does Table 6.2 tell us about the level of partisanship in Senate votes on Supreme Court nominees since 1975?

8 Why is the Kagan for Stevens switch unlikely to change the ideological balance of the Supreme Court to any great extent?

The Supreme Court, 2009–10

What you need to know

- The Supreme Court is the highest federal court in the USA.
- Of the nine justices who served in the term we consider in this chapter, six were appointed by Republican presidents and only three by Democrats.
- The Supreme Court has the power of judicial review. This is the power to declare acts of Congress or actions of the executive branch — or acts or actions of state governments — unconstitutional, and thereby null and void.
- By this power of judicial review, the Court acts as the umpire of the Constitution and plays a leading role in safeguarding Americans' rights and liberties.

The 2009–10 term of the Supreme Court was noteworthy for being the first in which Justice Sonia Sotomayor replaced Justice David Souter. Souter, appointed by Republican president George H. W. Bush in 1990, served for 19 years on the Court, retiring in 2009. Although he was appointed by a Republican, Souter had turned out to be a reliably liberal voice on the Court. It was therefore expected that Justice Sotomayor would follow mostly in the footsteps of her predecessor and that her appointment would not mark any significant shift in the philosophical balance of the Court. Was that indeed the case?

The session will be remembered for the Court handing down a landmark First Amendment freedom of speech decision — on campaign finance. The Court also handed down significant decisions on freedom of religion, gun control, and the rights of arrested persons, all by margins of 5–4 (see Table 7.1).

Table 7.1 Significant Supreme Court decisions, 2009-10 term

Case	Concerning	Decision
Citizens United v *FEC*	Campaign finance (First Amendment)	5–4
Salazar v *Buono*	Freedom of religion (First Amendment)	5–4
McDonald v *City of Chicago*	Gun control (Second Amendment)	5–4
Berghuis v *Thompkins*	Rights of arrested persons (Fifth Amendment)	5–4

The 2009–10 term

Freedom of speech — campaign finance

'Justices turn minor movie case into a blockbuster' was how the *New York Times* headlined its lead story when the Supreme Court issued its judgement in *Citizens United* v *Federal Election Commission* in late January 2010. It was, indeed, a blockbuster in terms of its scope and its significance, but its origins were modest. The case centred on a 90-minute film made about Hillary Clinton in 2008 while she was a candidate for that year's Democratic presidential nomination. The film was made and aired by a conservative interest group, Citizens United, and was naturally enough highly critical of the former first lady. The lower federal courts decided that the film fell foul of the 2002 Bipartisan Campaign Reform Act, commonly known as the McCain–Feingold Act, which forbade corporations, labour unions and special interest groups from using money from their general funds for 'any broadcast, cable or satellite communications' that refer to a candidate for federal office during the election season.

Unusually, when the case reached the Supreme Court in 2009, the justices decided not merely to consider the specifics of the case, but to broaden the scope of the case to include constitutional questions regarding freedom of speech in the First Amendment raised in a 1990 decision, *Austin* v *Michigan Chamber of Commerce*. In that case, the Supreme Court upheld the power of both the federal and state governments to restrict corporate involvement in political campaigns, ruling that corporations may be prohibited from spending money from their general funds to support or oppose political candidates. The 2010 decision reversed not only the 1990 decision, but also reversed a significant part of the Court's 2003 ruling in *McConnell* v *Federal Election Commission*, in which the Court had, just 7 years earlier, upheld the central provisions of the McCain-Feingold law. In that 5–4 decision, the majority was formed by liberal justices John Paul Stevens, David Souter, Ruth Bader Ginsburg and Stephen Breyer, joined by swing justice Sandra Day O'Connor. This 2010 decision is a clear indication, therefore, of just how much the Court has changed in those 7 years.

In its 5–4 decision in *Citizens United* v *FEC*, the Court's conservative majority — Chief Justice John Roberts, joined by Antonin Scalia, Clarence Thomas, Samuel Alito and Anthony Kennedy — ruled that when it comes to rights of political speech, corporations have the same rights as individuals. That overturned federal laws and Court decisions going back to the 1947 Taft-Hartley Act, which had prohibited trade unions from contributing money to federal election campaigns. Writing for the majority, Justice Kennedy made a bold and spirited defence of First Amendment rights:

> When government seeks to use its full power, including the criminal law, to command where a person may get his or her information or what distrusted

source he or she may not hear, it uses censorship to control thought. This is unlawful. The First Amendment confirms the freedom to think for ourselves.

Justice John Paul Stevens, in what was to prove to be his final term on the Court, wrote for the minority — the Court's liberal quartet — calling the decision 'a radical change in the law' that ignores 'the overwhelming majority of justices who have served this court.' Stevens, in a 90-page dissent, was critical of the scope of the decision as well as what he saw as its likely effect:

> Essentially, five justices were unhappy with the limited nature of the case before us, so they changed the case to give themselves an opportunity to change the law.

Stevens even went so far as to claim that the chief justice and those who joined him in the majority had an 'agenda' to overturn both legislative acts and court precedents. In his confirmation hearings back in 2005, the chief justice had denied having any such agenda and likened his new role to that of an umpire, stating to the Senate Judiciary Committee:

> Judges are like umpires. Umpires don't make up the rules; they apply them. The role of an umpire and a judge is critical. They make sure everybody plays by the rules. But it is a limited role. Nobody ever went to a ball game to see the umpire. I come before this committee with no agenda. I have no platform. Judges are not politicians who can promise to do certain things in exchange for votes.

Roberts had pledged to respect precedent set by the Court's previous decisions — what in legal language is called *stare decisis*, best translated from the Latin as 'to stand by that which is decided'. Roberts bristled at Stevens's charge that those in the majority could not be 'serious about judicial restraint'. After all, the concept of judicial restraint is one which defers to the directly elected legislative branch and places great stress on precedent established in previous Court decisions. Roberts defended himself by stating that *stare decisis* cannot be seen as appropriate to every decision. 'If it were,' he continued, 'segregation would still be legal'.

But there seems no doubt that this landmark judgement laid the five-member majority in this case open to criticism. This is how Stuart Taylor saw things in his column in the *National Journal* ('Conservatives forfeit high ground on activism', 22 January 2010):

> For decades conservatives have accused liberal Supreme Court majorities of judicial activism, by which I mean sweeping aside democratically adopted laws and deeply rooted societal traditions to impose their own policy preferences based on highly debatable interpretations of the Constitution's language and established meaning. On Thursday, the five more conservative justices forfeited whatever high ground they once held in the judicial activism debate. The majority's sweeping and unprecedented interpretation

of corporations' First Amendment rights wiped out federal laws dating back 63 years and two major [Supreme Court] precedents.

The usually placid President Obama was clearly angered by the sweep of the Court's decision. Speaking on the day the Court's decision was announced, the president declared:

It is a major victory for big oil, Wall Street banks, health insurance companies and the other powerful interests that marshal their power every day in Washington to drown out the voices of everyday Americans.

And the president hadn't finished. Six days later, in his State of the Union Address to a joint session of Congress, Obama issued another broadside to the Court:

Last week, the Supreme Court reversed a century of law that I believe will open the floodgates for special interests — including foreign corporations — to spend without limit in our elections.

Justice Samuel Alito, one of the six justices in the audience, was caught by television cameras shaking his head and mouthing the words 'not true'. Supreme Court justices make for an awkward sight at the State of the Union — seated in the front row, stony-faced, hands folded while members of Congress around them clap and cheer the president's carefully-crafted applause lines. But some thought that the president had on this occasion overstepped the mark of politeness. By all means criticise the Court's decisions, but not in public to their face in a forum which clearly offers them no opportunity of reply.

Two months later, in a question-and-answer session with law students at the University of Alabama, Chief Justice Roberts was asked whether it was right for the president to 'chide' the Court for its decision at the State of the Union. In what appeared to be a carefully crafted answer, Roberts began his reply:

First of all, anybody can criticise the Supreme Court without any qualm. Some people, I think, have an obligation to criticise what we do, given their office, if they think we've done something wrong. So I have no problems with that.

But then Roberts addressed the issue of the forum in which this incident had occurred — the sight of all the Democrat members of Congress jumping to their feet to applaud the president's criticism of the Court's decision in this case:

On the other hand, there is the issue of the setting, the circumstances and the decorum. The image of having the members of one branch of government standing up, literally surrounding the Supreme Court, cheering and hollering while the Court — according to the requirements of protocol — has to sit there expressionless, I think is very troubling.

Finally, the chief justice hinted that he and some of his colleagues would now rethink whether or not it is appropriate for them to continue to attend this event in future years:

> To the extent the State of the Union has degenerated into a political pep rally, I'm not sure why we're there.

For many years, Justice Stephen Breyer was the only member of the Court to attend. In all his 19 years on the Court, Justice David Souter (1990–2009) never attended. Watch out for who turned up at the State of the Union in January 2011.

Freedom of religion

Another hot-button issue upon which the Court has made a number of controversial rulings in recent years is the interpretation of the First Amendment's protection of freedom of religion. Liberal justices have tended to see a clear wall of separation between church and state, while conservative justices have tended to leave things up to state and local jurisdictions, even where that led to a blurring of this separation.

In *Salazar* v *Buono*, the Court overturned an objection to a cross that had been erected on public land in California as part of an area set aside to honour American servicemen killed in action during the First World War. Here was another 5–4 decision, another in which the conservative quartet of Roberts, Scalia, Thomas and Alito were joined by swing justice Kennedy, and another in which Kennedy wrote the majority opinion. 'The Constitution does not oblige government to avoid any public acknowledgement of religion's role in society', argued Justice Kennedy for the majority. To Kennedy, the cross 'is not merely a reaffirmation of Christian belief' but a symbol 'often used to honour and respect' heroism.

But in his dissent, Justice Stevens disagreed, stating that 'the cross is not a universal symbol of sacrifice; it is the symbol of one particular sacrifice, and that sacrifice carries deeply significant meaning for those who adhere to the Christian faith.' Therefore, in his view, and in the view of his three liberal colleagues — Breyer, Ginsburg and Sotomayor — it was an inappropriate symbol for the state to use to recognise war heroism.

Gun control

In *McDonald* v *City of Chicago*, the Court declared that the Second Amendment gives to Americans a fundamental right to bear arms and that the Due Process Clause of the Fourteenth Amendment means that this right cannot be infringed by state or local governments. This was a follow-up to the Court's 2008 ruling in *District of Columbia* v *Heller* which had made a similar ruling regarding the federal government, as Washington DC is governed by legislation passed by Congress.

But the *McDonald* decision was more symbolic than substantive. The Court's decision fell short of striking down the handgun ban in Chicago; in the words of Chicago Mayor Richard Daley, it merely makes the 28-year-old law 'unenforceable'. Here was another 5–4 decision with the conservatives, plus Kennedy, making up the majority. Justice Stevens, again in the role of dissenter, objected to the ruling saying that its vagueness will merely 'invite an avalanche of litigation that could mire the federal courts' for years to come.

Rights of arrested persons

In a landmark decision back in 1966 in *Miranda* v *Arizona*, the Supreme Court had stated that the Fifth Amendment's guarantee of the right to silence extended to the right of arrested suspects to be reminded of this right. In *Berghuis* v *Thompkins*, the Court ruled that criminal suspects, when given this verbal reminder by law enforcement officers, must say that they want to remain silent.

The case involved a Michigan suspect, Van Chester Thompkins, who had been arrested on suspicion of the murder of a youngster in a local shopping mall. Thompkins, having been read his rights, did not say that he wanted the questioning to stop; he merely remained silent while detectives conducted what was virtually a monologue in front of him for nearly 3 hours. At that point, one of the detectives asked Thompkins whether he believed in God, and a follow-up question, 'Do you pray to God to forgive you for shooting that boy down?' Thompkins answered 'yes' and then looked away. This one-word answer was used against him in his trial.

After his conviction, Thompkins claimed that his Fifth Amendment right to silence had been violated, and the federal appeals court agreed, stating that Thompkins's prolonged silence 'offered a clear and unequivocal message to the officers: Thompkins did not wish to waive his right' to remain silent.

But writing for the Court's five-member majority, Justice Anthony Kennedy disagreed:

> If Thompkins wanted to remain silent, he could have said nothing in response to [the detective's] questions, or he could have unambiguously invoked his Miranda rights and ended the interrogation. The fact that Thompkins made a statement about three hours after receiving a Miranda warning does not overcome the fact that he engaged in a course of conduct indicating waiver.

Kennedy was again joined by the Court's four conservatives. Newly-appointed justice Sonia Sotomayor, a former prosecutor whom some had thought might therefore be less protective of the rights of suspects, sided with her liberal colleagues calling the decision 'a substantial retreat from the protection against compelled self-incrimination'.

Court statistics

In the 2009–10 term, the Supreme Court delivered 86 opinions — the most for over a decade and a 28% increase on the 67 opinions delivered in 2007–08. This also indicates a steady increase since John Roberts succeeded William Rehnquist as chief justice in 2005. Of these 86 opinions, just 16 (19%) were 5–4 decisions, significantly down on the figure of 31% in the previous term (see Table 7.2). However, these 5–4 decisions once again showed very clearly the ideological divide within the Court. In 11 of these 16 decisions (69%), all four members of the Court's conservative wing (Roberts, Scalia, Thomas and Alito) were on one side and all four of the Court's liberal wing (Stevens, Ginsburg, Breyer and Sotomayor) were on the other. Between them was swing justice Anthony Kennedy. He joined the conservatives eight times and the liberals three times.

Table 7.2 Supreme Court statistics, 2004–10

	2004–05	2005–06	2006–07	2007–08	2008–09	2009–10
Number of opinions	74	69	68	67	74	86
Decided by 5–4	30%	23%	35%	17%	31%	19%
Justice most frequently in the majority	Breyer	Roberts	Kennedy	Roberts	Kennedy	Roberts Kennedy
Justice most frequently in the minority	Stevens	Stevens	Stevens	Thomas	Stevens	Stevens

The distinction for the justice most frequently in the majority during this term was shared between Chief Justice John Roberts and Associate Justice Anthony Kennedy. In the four previous terms, either Roberts or Kennedy had held this distinction. In the 2009–10 term, both Roberts and Kennedy were in the majority in 78 of the 86 decisions, that is in 91% of cases. They were followed in third place by Scalia and Alito, both in the majority in 87% of cases. So the conservatives yet again dominated the Court in this term. The justice least often in the majority was Justice Stevens — the sixth time in the last seven terms that he has been in that position.

The two justices most frequently in agreement were justices Ruth Bader Ginsburg and first-termer Sonia Sotomayor. They agreed on 90% of all decisions. (Roberts and Alito, who have held this distinction for three out of the four previous terms, managed only an 88% agreement rate.) It is worth looking in a little more detail at Justice Sotomayor's record in her first term. Table 7.3 shows her level of agreement with her eight colleagues during her first term. This shows that she agreed with Ginsburg and Breyer more frequently than with Stevens. Stevens was widely considered to be more liberal than Ginsburg and Breyer.

Table 7.3 Justice Sotomayor's level of agreement with fellow justices, 2009–10

Justice	Agreement with Sotomayor (%)
Ruth Bader Ginsburg	90
Stephen Breyer	90
John Paul Stevens	84
Anthony Kennedy	78
John Roberts	78
Antonin Scalia	69
Clarence Thomas	69
Samuel Alito	69

The Roberts Court

As we have just seen, Chief Justice Roberts was one of the two justices most frequently in the majority during 2009–10 — the third term that he has gained the top spot of the five he has served. 'The Roberts Court comes of age', was the headline of Adam Liptak's end of term article in the *New York Times* (29 June 2010), while the same paper's editorial called it 'The Court's aggressive term' (4 July 2010). 'Assertive', 'controversial', 'rash', 'aggressive', 'surprising', 'groundbreaking', 'the least deferential Court since the New Deal' are all descriptions made of the Court during this term. No judicial modesty or minimalism here: the new Roberts Court is often bold and its decisions far-reaching.

In the view of many commentators, Chief Justice Roberts, who joined the Court 5 years ago, took control of it this year, pushing hard on issues of concern to him — campaign finance, gun rights and criminal procedure. 'More than in any other year since he became chief justice, this has truly become the Roberts Court', commented Gregory Garre, a former solicitor general in the George W. Bush administration.

Court watchers are asking where the Roberts Court will turn its attention next. It indicated in this year's decisions that it is not yet finished with such issues as campaign finance and gun control. It is also likely to return to issues regarding church and state as well as capital punishment in future terms. But what will it do regarding recent legislation overhauling financial regulation and the healthcare system when they reach the Court?

The most conservative Court in decades?

In a *New York Times* article (24 July 2010), Adam Liptak claimed that the Supreme Court under Chief Justice Roberts 'is the most conservative in decades'. Among his reasons for making this claim, two in particular stand out. First, in its first 5 years (2005–10), the Roberts Court issued decisions that could be called conservative 58% of the time. In the 2008–09 term, this figure rose to 65%, the highest number in any year since 1953 — the year which ushered in the Warren Court under Chief Justice Earl Warren. The

Warren Court (1953–69) issued conservative decisions only 34% of the time. Both the Burger Court (1969–86) and the Rehnquist Court (1986–2005) issued conservative decisions 55% of the time. The upturn in conservative decisions, therefore, under Roberts has been quite significant.

Second, four of the six most conservative justices of the 45 who have sat on the Court since 1937 are still serving today: Chief Justice Roberts along with Justices Alito, Scalia and Thomas. It is even more startling to discover that Justice Kennedy — the so-called swing justice on the Roberts Court — is in the top ten of most conservative justices since 1937.

Critics of the Roberts Court have also accused it of practising judicial activism. The two main characteristics of judicial activism are the striking down of laws and the overruling of precedents, but as Tables 7.4 and 7.5 show, the Roberts Court has in fact been less activist than its predecessors, both in terms of laws struck down and precedents overruled. The most activist court in recent decades in those terms was the Burger Court. These tables also show, however, that although less activist than its predecessors, the Roberts Court has been much more conservative on those occasions when it has struck down a federal or state law, or overruled precedent. This was clearly shown in the landmark 2010 case of *Citizens United* v *Federal Election Commission*.

Table 7.4 Average number of laws struck down per term, 1953–2010

Court/dates	Laws struck down (average per term)	% conservative decisions
Warren Court (1953–69)	7.9	9%
Burger Court (1969–86)	12.5	12%
Rehnquist Court (1986–2005)	6.2	28%
Roberts Court (2005–)	3.0	60%

Source: *New York Times*, 24 July 2010

Table 7.5 Average number of precedents overruled per term, 1953–2010

Court/dates	Precedents overruled (average per term)	% conservative decisions
Warren Court (1953–69)	2.7	9%
Burger Court (1969–86)	2.8	47%
Rehnquist Court (1986–2005)	2.4	60%
Roberts Court (2005–)	1.6	88%

Source: *New York Times*, 24 July 2010

Justice John Paul Stevens, who retired at the end of this term, apparently had his own way of assessing the Court's conservative swing during his 35-year term of office. In an interview that he gave in April 2010, just 2 months before his retirement, Stevens claimed that all of the 11 justices who had joined the Court since 1975, including himself, were more conservative than his or her predecessor, with the possible exceptions of Ruth Bader Ginsburg (1993) and Sonia Sotomayor (2009).

In his article, Adam Liptak pointed out that while Chief Justice Roberts has not so far served anything like as long as his three immediate predecessors, 5 years of data on the Roberts Court are now available, 'and they point almost uniformly in one direction: to the right.'

Questions

1 What made *Citizens United* v *Federal Election Commission* a 'blockbuster' of a decision?
2 How did this case show the importance of the changed membership of the Court since 2003?
3 What criticisms did Justice Stevens make of this decision? Why was he especially critical of Chief Justice Roberts's decision in this case?
4 How did Roberts answer such criticism?
5 Why did Stuart Taylor claim that as a result of this decision, the conservative justices on the Court have 'forfeited whatever high ground they once held in the judicial activism debate'?
6 What was President Obama's reaction to this decision?
7 What was controversial about Obama's comments at the 2010 State of the Union Address?
8 How important a role did Justice Kennedy play in the four decisions considered in this chapter?
9 What do the data in Tables 7.2 and 7.3 tell us about the 2009–10 term?
10 What evidence do Tables 7.4 and 7.5 give that the Roberts Court is 'the most conservative Court in decades'?

Chapter 8

The Tea Party movement

The Tea Party movement has been one of the most extraordinary, unusual and confusing phenomenon to hit American politics in decades. Not since the birth of political action committees back in the 1970s has the landscape of American politics seen a new player on the scene of such potential significance. In this chapter, we will answer a number of key questions about the Tea Party movement and its supporters:

- How did it start?
- Who are they?
- What do they think?
- What do they want?
- Are they Republicans by another name?
- Will it work?

How did it start?

Even the name is odd. The movement takes its name from the so-called Boston Tea Party of 1773, a protest by American colonials against what they viewed as unfair taxation imposed on them by the British government — taxation without representation. In protest against the tax on tea, some angry Bostonians tipped more than 300 chests of tea from three vessels moored in Boston harbour into the sea on 29 November 1773.

The modern Tea Party movement took its name both to ally itself with the anti-big government sentiments of the original tea partiers, and because the word 'tea' serves as an acronym for their rallying cry — **T**axed **E**nough **A**lready'. The movement came into existence as a grass roots — bottom-up, rather than top-down — organisation, following the legislation Congress passed in reaction to the economic downturn, the banking collapse and the meltdown on Wall Street. Specifically, the Tea Party movement opposed the passage of such legislation as the Emergency Economic Stabilisation Act of 2008 (commonly known as the bank bailout scheme) and the American Recovery and Reinvestment Act of 2009 (commonly known as Obama's economic stimulus package).

The crowds at the early Tea Party rallies were small but gradually grew larger. By the summer of 2009, Tea Party activists were turning up at town hall meetings to shout down members of Congress who were trying to rally public support for the president's healthcare reform bill. Thousands of them then

turned up in Washington DC on 12 September 2009 for a rally on the National Mall. To the Tea Party movement, all these pieces of legislation were examples of unwanted 'big government' — whether sponsored by a Republican president (Bush's bank bailout) or by a Democrat.

The first National Tea Party Convention was held in early February 2010 in Nashville, Tennessee, with speakers including the former Republican vice-presidential nominee Sarah Palin. By then, the Tea Party movement had become so significant that political commentators were beginning to ask what effect it would have on the upcoming mid-term elections of 2010, as well as on the run-up to the 2012 presidential election. Because of its right-wing ideology, it was specifically being asked what effect, if any, the movement might have on Republican Party politics. Would the Republican Party seek to keep its distance from the movement, or would it seek to woo its support? Would Tea Party activists feel naturally drawn to the Republicans or would they seek to change the Republican Party into a more ideological party?

In April 2010, a *CBS News/New York Times* poll was commissioned to find out the answers to three questions about the Tea Party movement:
- Who are they?
- What do they think?
- What do they want?

Who are they?

The *CBS News/New York Times* poll found that 18% of Americans say that they are supporters of the Tea Party movement, but what that means is not at all clear. Given the movement's a bottom-up organisation, this probably means no more than 18% of Americans have a certain degree of sympathy with the movement, visit the website and follow news about it on television. It does not mean that 18% of Americans have attended a rally or donated money to the Tea Party movement. Indeed, among those 18% who called themselves supporters, a mere 13% had attended a rally, and only 2% had donated money.

From Table 8.1 we can make up a picture of the typical Tea Party supporter: a middle-aged, white male; quite likely to be a southerner; someone who is neither especially rich nor poor; a conservative who identifies himself either as a Republican or an Independent; a Protestant by religion and more likely to be a weekly attender at religious services than ordinary Americans; and likely to be a gun owner.

Tea Party types

Just as there are numerous types of tea, so there are different types of Tea Party. This is what is so confusing about the whole Tea Party thing: it's not an organisation, it's more of a non-organisation — highly decentralised and almost leaderless. It has no offices, no headquarters. It's based in activists' homes, on their laptops, iPhones and Blackberries. As Jonathan Rauch remarked in a recent *National Journal* article ('Group think', 11 September 2010):

> Strange though it may seem, this is a coordinated network, not a hierarchy. There is no chain of command. No group or person is subordinate to any other. The tea parties are jealously independent and suspicious of any efforts at central control.

Table 8.1 Who are the Tea Party supporters?

Group	Among Tea Party supporters (%)
Men	59
Women	41
Aged under 45	23
Aged over 45	75
Aged over 65	29
White	89
Black	1
Asian	1
Other	6
Northeast	18
Midwest	22
South	36
West	25
Educated only at high school	29
Some college education	33
College graduate	37
Earn less than $50K per year	35
Earn more than $50K per year	56
Earn over $100K per year	20
Republican	54
Democrat	5
Independent	41
Conservative	73
Liberal	4
Moderate	20
Protestant	61
Evangelical	39
Catholic	22
Other	6
None	7
Attend religious services weekly	38
Gun in household	58

Tea partiers believe that it is centralisation, leadership and top-down organisation that are at the root of the problems in Washington DC and in the national political parties. They want to avoid being tainted by the same diseases. Think of them as a kind of political form of Wikipedia — their units are self-funded and their members mostly work for free. (You don't get paid for writing entries for Wikipedia.)

It is hardly surprising therefore that Washington insiders, the press, politicians and lobbyists, all of whom work on a 'who's-in-charge' basis, find the Tea Party movement thoroughly confusing. 'Perplexed journalists looking for Tea Party leaders, is like someone asking to meet the boss of the internet', commented Jonathan Rauch in the same article. As Box 8.1 shows, the Tea Party movement is something like a confederacy — a loose collection of independent bodies who don't always agree among themselves.

Box 8.1 A brief guide to Tea Party groups

- **Tea Party Nation:** this group held the first ever Tea Party convention in February 2010 and will hold another in 2011
- **Tea Party Patriots:** the movement's largest membership organisation
- **Tea Party Express:** a political action committee which has sponsored bus tours, drawing thousands to local rallies and building local membership, as well as spending money on behalf of conservative candidates
- **National Tea Party Federation:** a discussion forum for Tea Party organisers; coordinates responses to attacks on the Tea Party movement
- **Americans for Prosperity:** trains activists in many states; organises rallies; spends money to air television issue ads
- **FreedomWorks:** advises members where to find local rallies and events; hosts activists for training seminars in Washington

Source: adapted from *National Journal*, 11 September 2010

What do they think?

Table 8.2 builds up an even more detailed picture both of Tea Party supporters and Tea Party activists — the latter being those who have attended a rally or donated money — in terms of what they think about various issues and people associated with government and politics in the United States.

Table 8.2 What do Tea Party supporters and activists think?

Characteristic	Tea Party supporters (%)	Tea Party activists (%)
Angry about Washington	53	72
Disapprove of job President Obama is doing	88	96
The economy is getting worse	42	62
Favourable opinion of the Republican Party	54	44
Favourable opinion of Glenn Beck	59	77
Favourable opinion of Sarah Palin	66	75
Palin has the ability to be an effective president	40	50
Violent action against government is justified	24	32
Get television political news from Fox News	63	77

We can see from these data that Tea Party supporters are: angry about Washington; overwhelmingly disapprove of the job Barack Obama is doing as president; have a favourable opinion of both conservative political commentator Glenn Beck and of 2008 Republican vice-presidential candidate Sarah Palin; and they tend to get their political news from watching Fox News. All these characteristics are even more true of activists than mere supporters.

A significant minority of each group — just under a quarter of supporters and just under a third of activists — think that violent action against government is justified. In this sense, Tea Partiers seem to be the political grandchildren of Barry Goldwater. Goldwater was the Republican presidential candidate in 1964 — he lost heavily to incumbent president Lyndon Johnson — who famously remarked in his acceptance speech at that year's Republican National Convention that 'extremism in the defence of liberty is no vice and… moderation in the defence of justice is no virtue!'

There are three areas in which Tea Party supporters and activists disagree somewhat. First, whereas only a minority (42%) of supporters think the US economy is getting worse, a majority (62%) of activists think that is the case. Second, whereas a minority (40%) of supporters think Sarah Palin would make an effective president, 50% of activists think she would. Third, whereas a majority (54%) of supporters have a favourable opinion of the Republican Party, only a minority (44%) of activists are of that view.

Having compared what Tea Party supporters think with what Tea Party activists think, we now turn to some comparisons between what Tea Partiers (supporters and activists) think compared with typical Americans (see Table 8.3). First, the data show that although a majority of Americans in April 2010 thought the country was 'on the wrong track' rather than 'heading in the right direction', this was much more pronounced among Tea Party supporters. Whereas 59% of Americans thought the country was 'on the wrong track', a whopping 92% of Tea Partiers were of that view.

Table 8.3 Views of ordinary Americans and Tea Party supporters compared

View	All (%)	Tea Party (%)
View of direction of the country:		
■ Right direction	34	6
■ Wrong track	59	92
View of things in Washington:		
■ Enthusiastic	5	1
■ Satisfied	26	4
■ Dissatisfied	48	41
■ Angry	19	53

The same was true when it came to views of the federal government. Whereas 67% of ordinary Americans were either dissatisfied or angry about Washington, that figure shot up to an incredible 94% among Tea Party supporters. The figures of those who described themselves as 'angry with things in Washington' were even more remarkable: just 19% of ordinary Americans, but 53% of Tea Party supporters.

If we look at what people think about President Obama we again see a clear distinction between average Americans and Tea Party supporters (see Table 8.4). Only 31% of Americans think that President Obama is 'very liberal'; a further 18% think he is 'somewhat liberal' but that still totals only 49%. Among Tea Party supporters, 77% think the president is 'very liberal', with a further 9% thinking he is 'somewhat liberal', totalling 86%. A surprisingly high percentage of Americans — 52% — think the president is 'moving the country towards socialism', but that figure rises to 92% among Tea Party supporters. And whereas a majority of ordinary Americans think that the president 'understands my needs and problems' (58%) and 'shares my values' (57%), only a small minority of Tea Party supporters — 24% and 20% respectively — hold these views about the president.

Table 8.4 Views on President Obama: ordinary Americans and Tea Party supporters compared

View	All (%)	Tea Party (%)
President Obama is:		
▪ Very liberal	31	77
▪ Somewhat liberal	18	9
▪ Moderate	28	7
▪ Conservative	10	1
Obama's policies are moving the country towards socialism:		
▪ Yes	52	92
▪ No	38	6
President Obama:		
▪ Understands my needs and problems	58	24
▪ Shares my values	57	20

Finally, what about the views of Tea Party supporters on Congress? How do they compare with the views of ordinary Americans? Again, as with the president, Tea Party supporters have a much more negative view than ordinary Americans. Now admittedly, even average Americans are not great admirers of Congress. Only 17% approve of the job Congress does while 73% disapprove. But among Tea Party supporters, the split is 1% to 96%. It's the same in answer to the question, 'Does Congress deserve re-election?' Among ordinary Americans, 78% said 'no'; the figure was 94% among Tea Party supporters. While Americans are negative about Congress, more (46%) approved of the job that their own representative was doing than disapproved (36%). Among

Tea Party supporters, 40% approved of the job done by their own representative but 49% disapproved.

Thus we can see that Tea Party supporters have an extremely negative view of Washington politicians — the president, Congress as a whole, and even their own representative.

What do they want?

In the 1976 classic movie *Network*, Peter Finch plays Howard Beale, a television newscaster who is so angry with the state of things in America that he invites his viewers to get up, open the window and shout: 'I'm as mad as hell, and I'm not going to take this anymore!' (You can see the 4-minute clip of Howard Beale's rant on **www.americanrhetoric.com**.) Tea Party supporters sometimes remind me of Howard Beale — they do often appear very angry. They're angry with the president, with Congress and with the federal government in general. But what do they want?

First and foremost, they want a smaller, more modest, more limited federal government. Asked 'How much has President Obama expanded the role of government in addressing economic problems?', 89% of Tea Party supporters answer 'too much'. Among ordinary Americans, the figure is 37%. Asked 'Which is more important: creating jobs through government spending or lowering the federal budget deficit?', 76% of Tea Party supporters say the latter. Among ordinary Americans, the figure is just 42%. Asked 'Which do you prefer: smaller government with fewer services or bigger government with more services?', 92% of Tea Party supporters say the former. Among ordinary Americans, the figure is 50%. It's probably true to say that Tea Party supporters' favourite modern president is Ronald Reagan. He shared their sceptical view of government (see Box 8.2).

Box 8.2 Ronald Reagan on the federal government

- 'Government does not solve problems, it subsidises them.'
- 'Government is like a baby: a mouth with a big appetite at one end, and no responsibility at the other!'
- 'The most terrifying words in the English language are: I'm from the federal government and I'm here to help.'
- 'The problem is not that people are taxed too little; the problem is that government spends too much.'
- 'If you invent a better mousetrap, the government comes along with a better mouse!'

There is no doubt that the Tea Party movement is much more concerned about economic matters than social ones. In this sense, its supporters are more like those who supported third party candidate Ross Perot in 1992 and 1996 than the social conservatives of the religious right. It was, after all, Perot who said:

The budget should be balanced, the treasury should be refilled, the public debt should be reduced and the arrogance of public officials should be controlled.

Most Tea Party supporters would agree with that. That said, Tea Party supporters do have some other concerns. Illegal immigration is one. When asked 'How serious a problem do you think the issue of illegal immigration is for the country right now?', 82% of Tea Party supporters said 'very serious', as against 60% of ordinary Americans. They are, on the other hand, highly sceptical about global warming as is shown in Table 8.5, with 65% of Tea Party supporters thinking that global warming will cause no serious impact or doesn't exist. The figure among ordinary Americans is just 28%.

Table 8.5 Views on the impact of global warming compared

Do you think global warming is an environmental problem that is causing a serious impact...?

	All (%)	Tea Party (%)
Now	38	12
In the future	29	19
No serious impact	23	51
Doesn't exist (volunteered)	5	15

A recent visit to the Tea Party Patriots website **www.teapartypatriots.org** gave a clue as to what Tea Party supporters want, with a page listing the movement's philosophy, core values and mission statement. The movement's philosophy is stated as follows:

Tea Party Patriots as an organisation believes in fiscal responsibility, constitutionally limited government, and free markets. Tea Party Patriots Inc. is a non-partisan grassroots organisation of individuals united by our core values derived from the Declaration of Independence, the Constitution of the United States of America and the Bill of Rights as explained in the Federalist Papers.

Box 8.3 details the movement's core values. The movement's mission statement is set out as follows:

To attract, educate, organise and mobilise our fellow citizens to secure public policy consistent with our three core values.

Republicans by another name?

Their plea for smaller and limited government, lower taxes and a belief in the 'original intent of the government our founders set forth' all sounds very like Republican Party politics and that is what the poll found. Indeed, 68% of Tea Party supporters vote 'always' or 'usually' for Republican candidates and a further 25% vote equally for candidates of both parties. Only 5% of Tea Party supporters vote 'always' or 'usually' for Democrat candidates. A more recent

Gallup survey (July 2010) concluded that Tea Party supporters' concerns are not decidedly different from those of Republican identifiers. The Gallup survey tested the views of Tea Party supporters and Republican identifiers on ten key issues (see Table 8.6) and found that 'the two groups differ only slightly in their views of federal government debt and the size and power of the federal government among the ten issues tested.'

Box 8.3 Tea Party Patriots' core values

Fiscal responsibility: Fiscal responsibility by government honours and respects the freedom of the individual to spend the money that is the fruit of his or her own labour. A constitutionally limited government, designed to protect the blessings of liberty, must be fiscally responsible or it must subject its citizenry to high levels of taxation that unjustly restrict the liberty our Constitution was designed to protect. The runaway deficit spending as we now see in Washington DC compels us to take action because we know that a heavy burden of national debt is a grave threat to our national sovereignty and the personal and economic liberty of future generations.

Constitutionally limited government: We are inspired by our founding documents and regard the Constitution of the United States to be the supreme law of the land. We believe that it is possible to know the original intent of the government our founders set forth, and stand in support of that intent. Like the founders, we support states' rights for those powers not expressly stated in the Constitution. As the government is of the people, by the people and for the people, in all other matters we support the personal liberty of the individual, within the rule of law.

Free markets: A free market is the economic consequence of personal liberty. The founders believed that personal and economic freedom were indivisible, as do we. Our current government's interference distorts the free market and inhibits the pursuit of individual and economic liberty. Therefore, we support a return to the free market principles on which this nation was founded and oppose government intervention into the operation of private business.

Source: **www.teapartypatriots.org**

Table 8.6 Views of issues as 'extremely serious threats' to the future wellbeing of the United States: Tea Party supporters and Republicans compared

Issues	Tea Party supporters (%)	Republicans (%)	Difference (% points)
Federal government debt	61	55	6
Size and power of federal government	49	43	6
Healthcare costs	41	37	4
Discrimination against minority groups	13	9	4
Illegal immigration	41	38	3
Environment/global warming	13	10	3
Unemployment	35	33	2
US action in Iraq/Afghanistan	24	22	2
Size and power of large corporations	16	14	2
Terrorism	51	51	0

Source: **www.gallup.com**

The problem, therefore, that the Republican Party faces is how to react to the Tea Party movement. Will its support help to give the Republicans the winning edge in upcoming election cycles, or will it prove to be an embarrassment, making it more difficult for Republicans to appeal to key moderate and independent voters? Even before the mid-term elections had got under way, there was plenty of evidence of Tea Party supporters' influence in the choosing of Republican senatorial candidates in Utah, Florida, Nevada, Alaska, Delaware and Kentucky. In Utah, Tea Party supporters were instrumental in the decision not to allow three-term Republican senator Bob Bennett to even be on the primary election ballot. And it was Tea Party supporters who were behind the choice of Marco Rubio as the Republican senatorial candidate in Florida — a decision that forced the Republican governor of the state, Charlie Crist, to run as an independent in the November election.

Will it work?

Tea Party supporters will answer this question with a resounding 'yes'. They are convinced that they have changed the landscape of politics for good — in both senses of the word — and that the Tea Party is here to stay. In his *National Journal* article, Jonathan Rauch states that there are some grounds for reaching this conclusion. Rauch points out that in several ways, the Tea Party movement resembles the highly successful group MoveOn.org. This began as a small online protest against President Clinton's impeachment back in 1998, but within a few years it was much better known — and highly successful — as a group opposing the war in Iraq. Both those issues have now passed, but the group still boasts 5 million members and is still, in Rauch's words, 'a potent political force, able to rapidly mobilise and target political protests and donations'.

There are many similarities between MoveOn.org and the Tea Party movement. Both emphasise people power as a remedy for flawed government. Both owe their influence to new media rather than old media. Both pride themselves on following rather than leading their memberships. But there are also significant differences which may lead us to question whether the Tea Party movement might run out of steam. Unlike MoveOn.org, the Tea Party movement has very little in the way of core, full-time staff. Whereas MoveOn.org concentrates its attention on national, winnable causes, the Tea Party movement is fragmented and appears to be more interested in ideological purity than political victory.

Being, as we have seen, a headless organisation, the Tea Party movement will find it much easier to stop something it doesn't like than agree on an alternative which it does like. That's fine in these early days when rock throwing is top of the agenda, but what if it had to build something, so to speak? Building a political alternative would almost certainly require compromise and negotiation, but with no leadership, who does that? And anyway, don't Tea Partiers think 'compromise' and 'negotiation' are dirty words?

It's also worth keeping in mind that the media may be prone to exaggerate the importance of the Tea Party movement. Here's E. J. Dionne, writing in the *Washington Post* in late September 2010 just after Tea Party candidates had scored upsets in some Senate primaries:

> Just recently, Tea Party victories in Alaska and Delaware Senate primaries shook the nation. In Delaware, Christine O'Donnell received 30,563 votes in the Republican primary, 3,542 votes more than moderate Rep. Mike Castle. In Alaska, Joe Miller won 55,878 votes for a margin of 2,006 over incumbent Sen. Lisa Murkowski. Do the maths. For weeks now, our national political conversation has been driven by 86,441 voters and a margin of 5,548 votes. A bit of perspective: When John McCain lost in 2008, he received 59.9 **million** votes.

Conclusion

During 2010, the Tea Party movement had a lot of fertile soil in which to grow: a Democrat president; two houses of Congress controlled by the Democrats; an economic recession; healthcare reform and illegal immigration much in the news. If the soil remains as fertile through 2011 and into 2012 then the Tea Party movement may yet remain a political force to be reckoned with.

Attracting Tea Party support in the mid-term elections in 2010 may have brought the Republican Party some welcome benefit, but what will the result of this be as the party tries to appeal to a larger — and therefore inevitably wider — electorate in 2012? A Republican Party that has no room for people such as Arlen Specter (defected to the Democrats), Bob Bennett (defeated for re-nomination in his Senate race in Utah in 2010), Charlie Crist (ran as an independent in Florida rather than face defeat in the Republican Senate primary by a Tea Party candidate), Lisa Murkowski and Mike Castle — both defeated in their Senate primaries by Tea Party-backed candidates — may not be one that is very attractive to moderate and independent voters, key blocs in winning *presidential* races.

Following the 2010 mid-term elections, Republican congressman Spencer Bachus of Alabama went so far as to suggest that it was Sarah Palin and the Tea Party movement who 'cost us control of the Senate'. That may or may not be true. But it is true to say that many Republicans will be asking how at least three Senate races were lost — in Delaware, Colorado and Nevada — because of the seeming ineptitude of Tea Party-backed candidates. It's a warning for what could happen in 2012.

Questions

1 Why is the movement called the Tea Party movement?
2 What is the profile of a typical Tea Party supporter?
3 How is the Tea Party movement organised?
4 What views does a typical Tea Party supporter hold?
5 What does Table 8.3 tell us about the views of Tea Party supporters compared with those of ordinary Americans?
6 What do Tea Party supporters think of (a) President Obama and (b) Congress?
7 What do Tea Party supporters want?
8 To what extent is it true to say that Tea Party supporters are really Republicans?
9 What difficulties does the Tea Party movement face?
10 What point was E. J. Dionne making in his *Washington Post* article? With hindsight, do you think this was a valid point?

The 2012 presidential election

What you need to know

- Presidential elections occur every 4 years.
- Both major parties hold a series of state-based primaries and caucuses during the first half of election year.
- Primaries and caucuses give ordinary voters a chance to say who they would like to see as the parties' presidential candidates.
- The 'invisible primary' is the period before the primaries and caucuses when would-be candidates try to position themselves for the race, gain name recognition and media attention, as well as raise large amounts of money.
- The candidate of each party who is ahead in the opinion polls at the end of the 'invisible primary' usually ends up as the party's presidential candidate.
- 'Front loading' is the term used to refer to the practice of many states to schedule their state primaries or caucuses as early as possible in election year.

The Democrats

Unlike 2008, the 2012 presidential election will almost certainly — baring some freak incident — see an incumbent president running for re-election. In that sense, 2012 will be more like 2004, 1996 and 1992 than the last presidential election. Incumbent presidents who want a second term are always re-nominated by their party, often without a contest. That was the case for George W. Bush in 2004 and Bill Clinton in 1996. Table 9.1 shows that over the past 56 years, nine presidents have sought a second term. Six were unchallenged for their party's nomination; all six were re-elected. During the same period, three were challenged for their party's nomination; all three lost their re-election bid. In 1976, President Ford was challenged by fellow Republican Ronald Reagan. Ford just won the nomination but lost the presidency to Democrat Jimmy Carter. Four years later, President Carter faced a challenge from fellow Democrat Edward Kennedy. Carter won the nomination but lost the presidency to Republican Ronald Reagan. In 1992, Republican President George H. W. Bush faced a challenge from fellow Republican and conservative commentator Pat Buchanan for his party's nomination. He won the nomination but lost the presidency to Democrat Bill Clinton.

Table 9.1 Incumbent presidents' re-election record since 1956

President	Party	Year	Significant primary challenger?	Re-elected?
Dwight Eisenhower	Rep	1956	No	Yes
Lyndon Johnson	Dem	1964	No	Yes
Richard Nixon	Rep	1972	No	Yes
Gerald Ford	Rep	1976	Yes	No
Jimmy Carter	Dem	1980	Yes	No
Ronald Reagan	Rep	1984	No	Yes
George H. W. Bush	Rep	1992	Yes	No
Bill Clinton	Dem	1996	No	Yes
George W. Bush	Rep	2004	No	Yes

Put simply, President Obama needs to avoid any serious challenge from within the Democratic Party in 2012. Provided he does, his chances for re-election are high. Since the turn of the twentieth century there have been 19 presidential elections featuring an incumbent president. In 14 (74%) of those, the president was re-elected; in only 5 was the president defeated — William Howard Taft in 1912, Herbert Hoover in 1932, Ford in 1976, Carter in 1980 and Bush in 1992. So the statistics suggest that President Obama ought to win a second term, especially as at the time of writing one cannot see any serious challenge to him from within the Democratic Party.

The Republicans

As in most elections featuring an incumbent president, all the initial attention will be on the challenging party — the Republicans in 2012. They have an open field with no incumbent president running. Often in such a situation as this, the front runner is a former vice-president: Al Gore for the Democrats in 2000, George H. W. Bush for the Republicans in 1988 and Walter Mondale for the Democrats in 1984. All three had previously served as vice-president, but one cannot envisage Dick Cheney running for the Republican nomination in 2012.

Inevitably, therefore, the party may look back to some of its unsuccessful candidates of 4 years ago, such as former governors Mitt Romney and Mike Huckabee. Some may even be touting the credentials of the 2008 vice-presidential candidate Sarah Palin. But others may be looking for new blood. We shall divide the field of prospective candidates into two groups — old and new, or if you prefer, has-beens and wannabes.

Someone old...?

Four prospective candidates come to mind at this stage who could be classified as 'old', both in terms of age and experience — they've all been around for some time. Indeed, two of them went round the course in the 2008 Republican primaries. **Mitt Romney**, who turns 64 in March 2011, was elected governor of Massachusetts in 2002 and served one 4-year term. When he ran for the party's presidential nomination in 2008, he won the primaries in Massachusetts,

Michigan, Montana and Utah, as well the caucuses in Wyoming, Nevada, Maine, Alaska, Colorado, Minnesota and North Dakota. He also came in a respectable second — behind the eventual nominee Senator John McCain — in key primaries in New Hampshire, Florida and California. Romney's greatest assets are his looks, his money, his experience and proven managerial competence. Romney has two significant drawbacks. First, he is a Mormon — a religious sect that many Americans still regard with some suspicion. Second, Romney is seen by many as a flip-flopper on key policies. Is he a liberal or a conservative? The way he has changed his position on such key social issues as abortion, gun control and gay rights makes him seem like an opportunist. But, at the time of writing, he's seen as the candidate to beat.

Another 2008 retread, and another former state governor, is **Mike Huckabee**, who was governor of Arkansas from 1996 to 2007. Huckabee, who turns 56 in August 2011, was the conservative's favourite in the 2008 primaries, having come to prominence with a sensational win in the Iowa caucuses. The trouble for Huckabee was that his Iowa victory was outdone by Barack Obama's defeat of Hillary Clinton in the Democrat caucuses on the same day. But Huckabee went on to win seven other contests — in Alabama, Arkansas, Georgia, Tennessee, West Virginia, Kansas and Louisiana. Huckabee's strengths are his evangelical Christian faith, his humour and his conservative credentials. His one big drawback is that he finds it difficult to be perceived as more than simply a regional candidate — appealing to folk only in the South.

Newt Gingrich, the former congressman from Georgia and speaker of the House of Representatives, has one big asset — name recognition. It was Gingrich who was the mastermind of the Republican Party's 'Contract with America' when the party swept to the majority in both houses of Congress in the 1994 mid-term elections — the first time it had controlled both houses of Congress for 40 years. In 1995, *Time* magazine named him their Person of the Year. But Gingrich brings baggage — his age (he will turn 68 in June 2011), his abrasive personality and the memory of the Republicans' overreaching during those heady days of the 1990s. Gingrich is like Marmite — you love him or you hate him.

The final feature in this foursome is **Haley Barbour**, the incumbent governor of Mississippi and former chairman of the Republican National Committee. Governor Barbour gained the national spotlight after Hurricane Katrina hit the state in August 2005 during his first term. His folksy style and managerial competence are clearly pluses. His drawbacks include his previous political life as a Washington lobbyist and his age (he turns 64 in October 2011).

Someone new...?
If Republicans want a younger candidate, someone who has not already been around for some time, then there are three potential candidates waiting in the wings, all of whom would be nearer 50 than 60 if inaugurated as president in

January 2013. Indeed, one would be nearer 40. A name to watch out for in 2012 is that of Senator **John Thune** of South Dakota. Thune was a member of the House of Representatives for 6 years (1997–2003) before being elected to the Senate in 2004 when he defeated the incumbent Democrat, and Senate majority leader, Tom Daschle. Thune is a true conservative and an evangelical Christian, making him attractive to many typical Republican primary voters. His electoral reputation was made by his David slaying Goliath act in 2004. Keep an eye out for John Thune. If not at the top of the ticket, he'd make an attractive running-mate in 2012, paving the way for a presidential bid in 2016 when he'd still be only 55.

Another name to watch out for is that of the incumbent governor of Minnesota, **Tim Pawlenty**. Pawlenty was widely tipped as a possible running mate for John McCain back in 2008. As the party's National Convention was being held in his home state that year, it would have been a popular choice. Pawlenty increased speculation that he would run for the presidency in 2012 when he announced back in 2009 that he would not seek re-election as governor in 2010. It is always thought to be a distinct advantage to run for the presidency when free from any other elective office. Pawlenty, a Polish American, will turn 51 in November 2011.

The youngest of all the potential candidates is another incumbent governor — **Bobby Jindal** of Louisiana. Jindal turns 40 in June 2011 and if elected to the presidency in 2012 would be the youngest ever president. Jindal served in the House of Representatives between 2005 and 2008 before being elected state governor in 2008 — the first Indian American to be elected as a governor of any state. In 2012, Jindal is probably more likely to be a vice-presidential candidate than to be at the top of the ticket.

Not forgetting…

The wild card has to be **Sarah Palin**, the former Alaska governor and 2008 running mate to John McCain. I still find it difficult to understand the Palin phenomenon. Why does someone who has so little experience of elective office and so little knowledge of national political issues have so much influence and such a following within the Republican Party? I have to admit to finding it difficult to take her seriously, seeing her more as a figure of fun — a kind of Attila the Hen. But maybe I'm just plain wrong on this one. After all, Palin did have a considerable influence in her endorsement of Republican candidates in the 2010 mid-term elections.

The nomination calendar

The Republicans' Delegate Selection Committee, which is in charge of recommending the calendar windows — that is, the dates before which and after which states may not hold their primaries and caucuses — appears likely to recommend that no contests be held before 1 February 2012, and that only Iowa, New Hampshire, Nevada and South Carolina be allowed to hold their contests before 1 March. If that calendar were adopted, it would mean the latest start to the presidential nominating contest since 1996, when Iowa held its caucuses on 12 February and the New Hampshire primary was held 8 days later (see Table 9.2).

Table 9.2 Dates of Iowa caucuses and New Hampshire primary, 1996–2012

Year	Date of Iowa caucuses	Date of New Hampshire primary
1996	12 February	20 February
2000	24 January	1 February
2004	19 January	27 January
2008	3 January	8 January
2012	6 February	14 February

One other change which the Republicans are considering is to insist that any state scheduling its primary before 1 April must allocate its convention delegates on a proportional, rather than a winner-take-all, basis. Democrats abolished winner-take-all primaries decades ago, but many state Republican parties — especially large population states — have stuck with them, believing that they increase their clout in the nominating process. Were the Republicans to insist on only proportional primaries up to the beginning of April, it would be much more difficult for any candidate to wrap up the nomination in the first 2 months of the contest. This would be to the advantage of lesser-known candidates such as John Thune and Tim Pawlenty, while it would disadvantage well-known and well-financed candidates such as Mitt Romney.

Meanwhile, the elaborately named Democratic Executive and Rules and Bylaws committees met in St Louis, Missouri, in mid-August 2010 to review their draft 'Call to the 2012 Democratic Convention'. Like the Republicans, the Democrats will permit Iowa, New Hampshire, South Carolina and Nevada to hold their contests in February, with all other states permitted to start no earlier than 1 March. The Democrats are also planning to award states holding their contests in April a bonus 10% in delegate numbers, with states holding off until May or June receiving a 20% bonus. The bonus delegate plan is an attempt to entice states away from front loading.

National Party Conventions

Being the challenging party, the Republicans will hold their convention first in 2012, with the Democrats following afterwards. The Republicans have already fixed both the date and the venue for their national convention in 2012 — 27–30 August in Tampa, Florida. For the Republicans, this will be the first Florida-based convention since the 1972 convention met in Miami Beach, and the first time ever in Tampa — for either party.

The Democrats have fixed the dates — 3–6 September — but have, at the time of writing, yet to finalise the venue. The two possible venues left in the running are St Louis, Missouri and Charlotte, North Carolina. With the Republicans opting for the crucial swing state of Florida, the Democrats may be tempted to do the same with Missouri. The last time the Democrats gathered in St Louis was in 1916 to re-nominate President Woodrow Wilson.

Electoral College votes

With the United States having conducted another decennial census in 2010, the 2012 presidential election will be the first to be conducted after the reapportionment of seats in the House of Representatives following that census. Changes in House seats mean changes in Electoral College votes. Some states will be gaining votes and others losing votes. By far the biggest winner is Texas (won by the Republicans in all the last eight elections) with four extra votes, taking its total to 38. The biggest losers are Ohio (won by the Democrats in three of the last five elections) and New York (won by the Democrats in all the last five elections), which will lose two votes each.

Clearly the changes in the Electoral College votes are going to favour the Republicans as they tend to win the states with the fastest growing populations — such as Texas, Arizona, Georgia and Utah. Likewise, the Democrats tend to win the states with the slowest growing populations — such as Ohio, New York, Massachusetts and New Jersey. If one re-run the 2008 election on the new Electoral College votes, the Republicans would have made an overall gain of six electoral votes. In other words, if the 2008 election had been run on the basis of 2012 figures, the result would have been an Obama win by 359–179 rather than 365–173. It's not a huge difference, but it's still significant.

Questions

1 What does Table 9.1 tell us about President Obama's likelihood of re-nomination and re-election in 2012?
2 What are the main strengths and weaknesses of Republicans Mitt Romney and Mike Huckabee?
3 Why is it suggested that Senator John Thune might be a strong Republican candidate?
4 What are the major parties planning to do to discourage 'front loading' in 2012?
5 Why are changes in Electoral College votes likely to favour the Republican Party in 2012?